WHO RULES AMERICA

The People
vs.
The Political Class

by Eric O'Keefe

The creation of the United States of America
is the greatest of all human adventures.

— Historian Paul Johnson

TABLE OF CONTENTS

THE KEYSTONE REFORM

A gulf separates the rulers from the ruled in our country. Soon it may be an unbridgeable chasm. Into the abyss will tumble our republic, the grand experiment in self-government conceived in liberty and consecrated by genius, experience, and the hard work of citizenship.

But it doesn't have to be this way.

The problem, quite simply, is that our representatives are not representative. They are a separate class, identifying their interests with those of the government, not the people. When the interests of the government in which they serve and the people they putatively serve conflict — as is the case with issues ranging from term limits to foreign policy — they invariably side with the government.

Nor do they believe that ordinary Americans are capable of the task of self-government. Henry Hyde, the Illinois Republican who has spent one-quarter of a century in the House of Representatives, declared his opposition to citizen government through term limits with: "I just can't be an accessory to the dumbing down of democracy. America needs leaders, it needs statesmen, it needs giants — and you don't get them out of the phone book."[1]

Here, indeed, is a man who has spent far too long within the cocoon of incumbency. Putting aside his curious scale of measurement — are Trent Lott and Richard Gephardt and Newt Gingrich and Tom Daschle really "giants"? — Hyde evidently views those of us outside his circle of 535 as mere names in a phone book: puny, nondescript, one indistinguishable from the next. The facts are quite different. Thousands of potentially outstanding representatives live in the towns and cities and villages of America. They enrich the civic life of their communities through service in Rotary Clubs, Sunday Schools, soup kitchens, Little Leagues, community theaters, and the countless other manifestations of good old American volunteerism.

Unlike the Hydes of Washington, they regard the goal of public service as something more than merely saving one's own hide.

We forget that our forefathers wanted the country to serve not as "the world's only superpower," but as a living example of a land whose government drew its breath from the consent of the governed. The

Founders envisioned a land in which the governors came from the ranks of the governed, and other citizens routinely took turns as legislators. John Adams said of the First Continental Congress in 1774, "I am for making of it annual, and for Sending an entire new set every Year, that all the principal Genius's may go to the University in Rotation — that We may have Politicians in Plenty."[2]

Those who were badly governed in other nations took heart from the American example. As the great pamphleteer and patriot Thomas Paine wrote in *Common Sense*:

> O! ye that love mankind! Ye that dare oppose not only the tyranny but the tyrant, stand forth! Every spot of the old world is overrun with oppression. Freedom hath been hunted round the globe. Asia and Africa have long expelled her. Europe regards her like a stranger, and England hath given her warning to depart. O! receive the fugitive, and prepare in time an asylum for mankind.[3]

In Paine's day, all other political questions were subordinated to the key issue of the age: who should rule Americans, a distant king or the elected representatives of American freemen? Paine, who was passionately anti-slavery — his work inspired the founding of America's first abolitionist organization — nevertheless worked closely with American patriots who owned slaves. The question of the moment was American independence, and Paine and others fought to answer it in a way that implied the eventual end of slavery with the pronouncement that "all men are created equal...."

We stand at a similar historical junction. Public confidence in the federal government is near record low levels. And the much-heralded Republican Revolution of 1994 failed to shake the power and complacency of the Incumbent Party. Those seeking an American restoration are coming to understand that it is not possible until we overthrow the political class and reinstitute a government of citizens.

Americans do not trust their own government. Indeed, many fear it as a threat to life, liberty, and property. When in 1964 the Roper polling organization asked Americans, "Do you think you can trust the government in Washington to do what is right most of the time?" 76 percent answered yes. Thirty-two years later, having weathered Vietnam,

Watergate, the Great Society, and scandals both petty and profligate, only 19 percent of our citizens answer in the affirmative.[4]

Pervasive cynicism about government dominates the American psyche. A 1998 poll by The Pew Research Center for the People and the Press found that an overwhelming majority (76 percent) say that elected officials in Washington quickly lose touch with the people they are supposed to represent.[5]

And that 76 percent cannot be caricatured as the "angry white men" who haunt the fevered dreams of the lords of the Potomac. In 1998 an obstetrician turned congressman, Rep. Tom Coburn (R-OK), in announcing that he would not serve beyond a third term, remarked, "After four years in Congress, I believe more than ever that our nation's problems have been created because career politicians have set themselves apart as an elite class of people trying to dictate to us how we run our lives."[6]

Congressman Coburn cut to the core of the current disenchantment. Who rules America? That is the real question underlying the term limits debate. Is it the people, or a self-selecting political class? And who *should* rule: the citizenry, represented by citizen-legislators who serve for a brief time and then return to the communities whence they came; or a small and protected class of careerist politicians?

The "world's only superpower" sets a powerfully bad example. And the harm that our bad example inflicts extends beyond such trivia as a few points in the Gross Domestic Product. Bad politics trumps technological innovation, improved transportation, medical advances, and faster communication. A century ago the world was at relative peace and democracy was on the march. Yet within two decades the European continent was encrusted with blood, her economies lying in shambles. The decimated countries proved fertile seedbeds for the growth of horrific totalitarian states, demonstrating the consequences of bad politics: death and destruction.

The atrocities of communism in our century are almost beyond reckoning. According to the best estimates, communist governments in the Soviet Union, Cambodia, China, and elsewhere killed at least 85 million people — an unfathomable number, really. Whether executed or starved to death, killed in gulags or in labor camps, these 85 million bear mute but overpowering testimony to the evils of the state as master.

Thankfully, we have been spared the carnage and gore that bloodied the killing fields of Europe and Asia. Communism and fascism never found fertile ground in these United States. As in Tom Paine's day, the rest of the world has seen our land as a beacon of liberty, ever beckoning and inspiriting the oppressed and downtrodden.

But that beacon shines dimly today. The problems that beset us seem insoluble and many Americans feel ashamed of their government. Given that the rest of the world has been governed less well — indeed, more brutally — than the United States of America, our current mess will have repercussions far beyond our shores.

Using raw numbers, the political state of the world is cause for cheer. The Communist Bloc lies in the dustbin of history, and Freedom House estimates that 118 of the globe's 193 recognized countries are "democratic" — an unprecedented proportion. Yet as Fareed Zakaria, managing editor of *Foreign Affairs,* has pointed out, the figures are deceiving. Most of the ostensibly "democratic" countries are illiberal, that is, they deny their citizens basic liberties. The mere right to vote means little if it is not undergirded by the right to dissent, the right to worship freely, the right to own property, the right to publish, and the right to free association.[7]

But we should be wary before we cast stones at imperfect democracies. Our own system is in a state of serious disrepair. Most congressional elections are so stacked in favor of the incumbent that they resemble the farcical contests found in sham democracies. The two-party system still exists, but instead of Democrats and Republicans, we have an Incumbent Party and a Party of the Rest of Us. We have the votes, but they have the power. And they have the effrontery to use our tax dollars to perpetuate their power.

Our bad example will influence fledgling democracies. Indeed, our tax dollars are used by such creatures of Washington as the National Endowment for Democracy to set up electoral systems (or interfere in internal affairs, depending on your point of view) in Third World nations. It is a safe bet that the National Endowment for Democracy (NED) is not giving tutorials on the virtues of rotation in office.

Term limits is not about "kicking the bums out." It is about restoring accurate representation. To call the Congress "the people's house," as was once common, is to invite snorts and jeers. The people may sit in the galleries for a few minutes before being ushered out, but it is a rare visitor who feels any more a sense of proprietorship in the U.S. House or Senate. Rather, he feels like a stranger in a strange land, a tourist catching a glimpse of some exotic ceremony to which he is not party. The Congress belongs to Them, not to We the People, and until we take it back we cannot begin to cure the various other maladies that afflict our land. Term limits must come first: *until our representatives become representative, we will remain in thrall to a political class that cannot and will not reform itself.* The institution must be reinvigorated, restored to its proper place in the political life of the American community, before we can effect any of the other necessary renewals in our beloved country.

So proponents of term limits are not a mob of disaffected rabble, scouring the ground for sticks and stones with which to clobber congressmen. The junkets, the venality, the occasional Honorable who is caught with his hand deep in the cookie jar are cause for concern, but they are not what motivates us. We are not in this to punish members of Congress or harass Washington monuments. Anger is not the presiding emotion within the term-limits movement. The real spur is love: love of country, love of community, and belief in the promise of the American Founding. We are keeping the faith of our fathers, reinfusing that faith into the political bloodstream. We seek to make America once more the last, best hope, the beacon of liberty to which the weary and oppressed can turn their hopeful eyes. We hope — we intend — to redeem the American promise.

CHAPTER ONE

"THE RULERS ARE THE SERVANTS": ROTATION IN OFFICE

The American system of limited constitutional government is based upon several familiar precepts: federalism, the separation of powers, frequent elections, and the system of checks and balances, to name a few. Most are codified in law, while others became hallowed through custom and usage. The Founders believed they need not be written into the Constitution, because their worthiness was so manifest that common practice would firmly establish them as de facto rules of the polity. The two-term limit on presidents, for instance, which George Washington established, was not proclaimed on paper until Franklin Roosevelt's four terms made necessary the Twenty-Second Amendment.

Rotation in office was also an essential feature of our government. Under the Articles of Confederation, the newly independent Americans limited delegates to Congress to no more than "three years in any term of six years": A Massachusetts delegate named Samuel Osgood holds the honor of being the first elected member of the national Congress to be booted from office by term limits.

Several of the states in revolutionary America limited terms by statute: the Declaration of Rights in the Massachusetts Constitution of 1780, for instance, required "public officers to return to private life" so as "to prevent those, who are vested with authority, from becoming oppressors."[1] Pennyslvania required rotation of legislators and executives to obviate "the danger of establishing an inconvenient aristocracy."[2] The Virginia Constitution of 1776 declared of officeholders that "they should at fixed periods, be reduced to a private station, [and] return into that body from which they were originally taken."[3]

Thus rotation in office is not a "new idea" cooked up by the think tanks in Washington and Northern Virginia: it is a venerable principle of republics, as has been shown in the pathbreaking work of political scientist Mark P. Petracca of the University of California-Irvine. Petracca has detailed the importance of rotation in the ancient republics of Athens, Rome, Venice, Florence...and the remarkable thing is that its champions across time and place have spoken in the same tongue. The Roman orator Cicero declared that "the man who obeys should have the hope that he will one day command, and he who commands should reflect that in a short time he will have to obey."[4] The Renaissance city-state of Venice required rotation on its council because "human nature is such that men cannot be trusted with long continuance in office of great power."[5]

Who will say that human nature has changed in the centuries since?

The utility of rotation in office was axiomatic to the Founding Fathers. It was basic to their personal and intellectual histories and a bedrock principle in the books and newspapers they read — like *Cato's Letters*.

Cato's Letters were the extraordinarily influential 18th-century pamphlets written by Englishmen John Trenchard and Thomas Gordon. They helped inspire the American Revolution. As the historian Clinton Rossiter wrote, "*Cato's Letters* was the most popular, quotable, esteemed source of political ideas in the colonial period."[6] These stirring pamphlets also contain some of the most eloquent arguments ever made on behalf of rotation in office.

Cato's Letter No. 60 advocates "changing [representatives] so often, that there is no sufficient time to corrupt them, and to carry the ends of that corruption."[7]

Trenchard and Gordon argue the point at length and with great wisdom in Letter No. 61:

> Men, when they first enter into magistracy, have often their former condition before their eyes. They remember what they themselves suffered with their fellow subjects from the abuse of power, and how much they blamed it; so their first purposes are to be humble, modest and just; and, probably, for some time, they continue so. But the possession of power soon alters and vitiates their hearts, which are at the same time sure to have leavened and puffed up to an unnatural size, by the deceitful incense of false friends and by the prostrate submission of parasites. First they grow indifferent to all their good designs, then drop them. Next, they lose their moderation: Afterwards, they renounce all measures with their old acquaintances and old principles, and seeing themselves in magnifying glasses, grow in conceit,

a different species from their fellow subjects. And so, by too sudden degrees become insolent, rapacious and tyrannical, ready to catch all means, often the vilest and most oppressive, to raise their fortunes as high as their imaginary greatness. So that the only way to put them in mind of their former condition, and consequently of the condition of other people, is often to reduce them to it, and to let others of equal capacities share the power in their turn. This also is the only way to qualify men, and make them equally fit for domination and subjection. A rotation, therefore, in power and magistracy, is essentially necessary to a free government.[8]

"Seeing themselves in magnifying glasses": has there ever been a better capsule description of Newt Gingrich and Richard Gephardt?

Cato's argument was typical, if unusually eloquent. The wisdom of rotation was not debatable to the Founders: it was truth. Benjamin Franklin knew it: "In free governments the rulers are the servants, and the people their superiors...For the former to return among the latter [does] not degrade, but promote them."[9] John Adams knew it. Representatives should be:

'Like bubbles on the sea of matter borne, They rise, they break, and to that sea return.' This will teach [representatives] the great political virtues of humility, patience, and moderation, without which every man in power becomes a ravenous beast of prey.[10]

Virginia statesman Richard Henry Lee knew it: "Even good men in office, in time, imperceptibly lose sight of the people, and gradually fall into measures prejudicial to them."[11] (The only Founding Father who did not esteem rotation was Alexander Hamilton, whose views were far from the mainstream of the Constitutional Convention. Hamilton proposed that both Senators and the President hold "their places during good behavior, removable only by conviction on impeachment for some crime or misdemeanor."[12] His views served as a prescient anticipation of Strom Thurmond, perhaps, but did not persuade his colleagues. His version of the Constitution was rejected.)

Note that in singing the praises of rotation in office, the Founders were not worried that evil men would get in office and stay. Rather, they feared that *normal* men who attained office would stay so long as to *become* bad. Rotation, like term limits, guards virtue by dampening the temptations of power-lust and careerism.

During the sweltering Philadelphia summer of 1787, when the Constititional Convention was drawing up what would become the most venerable compact of modern times, one matter upon which almost every delegate agreed was the desirability of rotation in office. The issue cut across the usual partisan lines dividing Federalist from Anti-Federalist, North from South, small state from large state. In Philadelphia and at the state ratifying conventions that followed, one consistent theme voiced by both sides in the ratification debate was that "the Representatives ought to return home and mix with the people" so as not to "acquire the habits of the [seat of government; it was not yet called Washington!] which might differ from those of their Constituents,"[13] as Roger Sherman of Connecticut argued. Sherman was nothing if not far-sighted. He understood that even the best-intentioned reformer will "go native" if he has too long a residence in the seat of power.

Nevertheless, the convention did not write term limits into the Constitution. The "Virginia Plan" first considered by the delegates contained term limits for members of the national legislature. In the end, the crafters of the Constitution thought they were unnecessary, given the general

U.S. House Turnover, 1790-1996

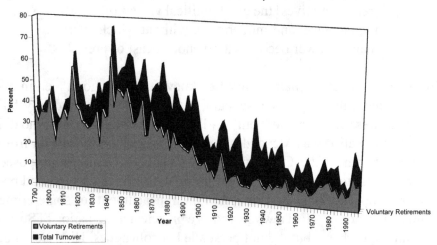

Sources: Gerald Benjamin and Michael J. Malbin, "Turnover Rates in the U.S. House and Senate, 1793-1990," in *Limiting Congressional Terms* and U.S. Term Limits.

acceptance of the rotation principle. Their absence from the document worried Thomas Jefferson, for one, who believed that the temptations of careerism might ultimately prove too strong to be reined in by custom and honor. He wrote James Madison about the Constitition: "The second feature I dislike, and strongly dislike, is the abandonment, in every instance, of the principle of rotation in office."[14] Another Virginia statesman, Richard Henry Lee, agreed: the lack of term limits in the Constitution was "highly and dangerously oligarchic."[15]

Jefferson and Lee's fears would seem unfounded, at first. The turnover rate in Congress ranged between 30 and 76 percent during the years 1790-1898. During one stretch (1842-1854), it did not fall below 50 percent. Ability, not seniority, determined one's position within the House. Henry Clay of Kentucky was elected Speaker on his very first day as a member of the House of Representatives.

With turnover rates robustly high throughout the 19th century, the number of House members who had served 12 or more years remained in the single digits for much of the century. It hit an antebellum high of 15 in 1811 (and this graybeard Congress elected neophyte Henry Clay Speaker) and never rose above that figure until 1887. As scholars from the Library of Congress have written, "it became customary to serve no more than four years in the House nor six in the Senate."[16] The great British historian James Bryce, in his magisterial book *The American Commonwealth* (1888), declared "Rotation in office was and indeed by most men still is, held to be conformable to the genius of democracy."[17]

The election of 1876, when our nation celebrated its centennial, returned to office a grand total of three House members who had served at least 12 years. The bicentennial election of 1976 returned 146, and by 1990 the number reached an incredible 198. By 1989, 92 percent of those taking the oath of office to serve in the U.S. House of Representatives had served in the body before. The House had become a virtual rest home for superannuated politicians.

The figures in the U.S. Senate are no less startling. Between 1789 and 1889, no Congress could boast even as many as ten senators with 12 or more years of service under their belt; by 1991 a dismaying 49 senators in that body of 100 had served 12 years or more and were making a career of it.

Clearly, the principle of rotation — a fundamental of the American order — had vanished.

The reasons for this were several: as the federal government swelled to an unimagined size, service therein became more attractive. Power — the chance to become one of those ravenous beasts of prey against which John Adams warned — proved an irresistible bait. Pensions expanded and opportunities to cash in on long-term congressional experience by becoming a lobbyist multiplied.

The system became sclerotic. Incumbents could not be dislodged: like diamonds, a congressional career was forever. In 1988, only six House incumbents and a single Senate incumbent were defeated — and most of this luckless septet were embroiled in scandal. Over the next couple of years a series of congressional outrages — the midnight pay raise, the House Bank overdraft scandal, malfeasance in the House Post Office, the savings and loan debacle — fed public disgust. By 1990, the average member of Congress had served more than ten years. In 1896 the average tenure had been 30 months, or barely more than one term. The cost that our republic had paid for discarding rotation in office was enormous and obvious: the solution, it became clear, was to bring back rotation. To honor the words of Andrew Jackson: "Every man who has been in office a few years believes he has a life estate in it, a vested right. This is not the principle of our government. It is a rotation in office that will perpetuate liberty."[18]

Term limits, which had lain dormant in a corner of the national attic for almost two centuries, revived. (The first term limits constitutional

Projected Turnover in the U.S. House of Representatives Under a Three Term Limit

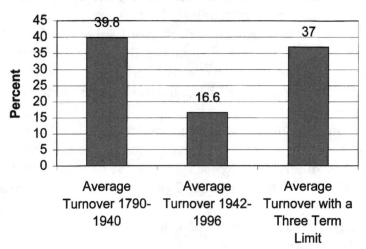

Sources: Gerald Benjamin and Michael J. Malbin, "Turnover Rates in the U.S. House and Senate, 1793-1990," in *Limiting Congressional Terms* and U.S. Term Limits.

amendment had been proposed in 1789 by South Carolina Congressman Thomas Tucker.) Presidents Harry Truman and Dwight D. Eisenhower advocated limiting congressional terms. But it took 98 percent reelection rates in the House and the manifest unwillingness of our career politicians to tackle tough issues to place term limits at the center of the national debate.

Harry Truman said that congressional term limits would "cure two maladies of democracy — legislative senility and seniority."[19] President Eisenhower concurred, telling a friend in a 1967 letter, "I am not enamored of the professional politician...I would rather see a flow of fresh blood constantly coming into Congress."[20] Their fellow Americans were coming to see the point.

CHAPTER TWO

"AN EXACT PORTRAIT OF THE PEOPLE AT LARGE": CONGRESS AS IT WAS INTENDED TO BE

The House of Representatives we are supposed to have bears so little resemblance to the House of Representatives we do have that one is reminded of the before and after photos advertising quack diet remedies in grainy tabloids, with the order of the photos reversed. The Founders did *not* envision a bloated, unresponsive body of virtually invulnerable career politicians. The House of Representatives was "the grand repository of the democratic principle of the government," wrote James Madison in his notes on the Constitutional Convention of 1787. As such, "it was given the prerogative of initiating all legislation on taxes, where sensitivity to popular sentiment was deemed especially important," writes Richard F. Fenno, dean of congressional scholars.[1]

This was no speculative endeavor. By 1763 the lower houses in every colony had taken control of government away from the royal governors. In *A History of the American People*, Paul Johnson writes that "This triumph of the popular system had one very significant consequence for everyday life. It meant that the mainland colonies were the least taxed territories on earth." Popular government "was a tremendous benefit which America carried with it into Independence and helps to explain why the United States remained a low-tax society until the second half of the twentieth century."[2]

The Revolution was fought to defend America from the English government's encroachment on the liberties protected by colonial legislatures. The Founders created the House of Representatives to assure the same protections for posterity.

In *The Federalist 52*, James Madison wrote,

> As it is essential to liberty that the government should
> have a common interest with the people, so it is par-
> ticularly essential that the branch of it under con-

sideration [the House of Representatives] should have an immediate dependence on, and an intimate sympathy with, the people.[3]

Today that essential dependence has been displaced by another kind of dependence: on the coffers of the state. Members of Congress gorge on the taxes we pay. The sympathy of which Madison spoke is nowhere in evidence, otherwise such overwhelmingly popular reforms as term limits would already be enshrined in the Constitution.

The House of Representatives was to be an "exact transcript" of American society. This is not to say that members would be mere robots, programmed by the folks back home to vote in precise accordance with their every wish and sentiment; but rather, that these would be men so well-grounded in the customs and mores of their districts, so emblematic of their constituencies, that they would unselfconsciously reflect the prevailing beliefs and attitudes of their neighborhoods. They would not be supermen, but they would be exemplary men: typical in their jealous regard of liberty, uncommon in their ability.

"Representatives," said George Mason at the Constitutional Convention, "should sympathize with their constituents; should think as they think and feel as they feel; and...for these purposes should even be residents among them."[4] The words "sympathy" and "sympathize" keep popping up. The dictionary defines sympathy as "mutual understanding or affection,"[5] and that can only be achieved, politically, by long years of living as neighbors. It cannot be manufactured by direct-mail vendors or slick TV commercials. To borrow Mr. Lincoln's formulation, the representative must be *of* the people before he can be *for* the people.

The Founders' intention was that representatives would reach the same policy conclusions as their constituents would have, had they given the same attention to the matter. In 1776, that most resonant of all American years, John Adams wrote of the legislature that the patriots soon would create:

> The principal difficulty lies, and the greatest care should be employed, in constituting this representative assembly. It should be in miniature an exact portrait of the people at large. It should think, feel, reason and act like them. That it may be the interest of

of the assembly to do strict justice at all times, it should be an equal representation, or, in other words, equal interests among the people should have equal interests in it. Great care should be taken to effect this, and to prevent unfair, partial, and corrupt elections.[6]

Legislators should "think, feel, reason and act" like the people at large. So why, 222 years later, are we discussing how to *make* Congress do what a majority of voters want it to do? Why, when public opinion polls show that upwards of three-quarters of Americans, including majorities of every racial, ethnic, religious, and sectional group, favor term limits on Congress — CBS News political director Martin Plissner said he has "never seen an issue on which there was so little demographic variation" — does that Congress "think, feel, reason and act" in direct opposition to the people who elected it?[7]

Self-preservation, one might answer. Yet this antithesis also exists over matters that have nothing to do with the number of years a person might occupy office. Take, for example, foreign aid. Set aside for the moment whether or not U.S. government subsidies to foreign governments are a good or a bad idea. A Congress motivated by Adamsonian principles would reflect, roughly, the attitudes of its constituents when ladling (or penny-pinching) such aid. Yet our Congress behaves in the opposite way.

For stark evidence, consider a 1997 survey of the Center for International and Security Studies at the University of Maryland. The pollsters asked members of Congress and their staffs to characterize the attitudes of the voters on such matters as the United Nations, U.S. intervention in foreign wars, and foreign aid.

The picture of the American electorate painted by the members and their staffs was that of a people who are overwhelmingly antiwar, hostile to foreign military involvements and foreign aid, and suspicious of the United Nations. For instance, 82 percent of the congressmen and 75 percent of the staffers agreed that the American people desired the U.S. to take a smaller role in the policing of the world. Eighty-two percent of the congressmen also characterized the attitude of the America people toward the United Nations as "negative." Eighty percent of the members said that Americans were opposed to U.S. involvement in "UN peacekeeping" missions — a loaded phrase in any event, as who can oppose peacekeeping? ("UN occupation armies" would be a no less accurate term.) Finally, zero percent — that is, not a single member in the interview sample — believed that Americans were "basically supportive" of foreign aid.[8]

These numbers indicate that our representatives are convinced that the people they represent do not want the U.S. government to send money or soldiers into foreign wars or UN military missions. They do not see a divided public but one united around what are often called "isolationist" policies. (These policies could be taken straight from President George Washington's Farewell Address. Washington did not seek to isolate his nation but merely to refrain from involvement in foreign quarrels. As he put it, "It is our true policy to steer clear of permanent alliances with any portion of the world...Harmony, liberal intercourse with all nations are recommended by policy, humanity, and interest." But the "great rule of conduct for us in regard to foreign nations is, in extending our external relations to have with them as little *political* connection as possible.")[9]

Even a cursory glance at the record of Congress over the last several years demonstrates that they do not "think, feel, reason and act" like the folks back home when it comes to matters abroad. There has been little congressional opposition to the unpopular deployment of U.S. troops in the UN missions in Haiti, Bosnia, and Somalia. Despite occasional grumbling from backbenchers, the U.S. commitment to the United Nations and its works remains as strong as ever. Far from disengaging and tending to problems at home, the U.S. government has its fingers in countless foreign pies. The people want withdrawal; their representatives know this, yet give them engagement. So what gives? (Other than the taxpayers and the parents of young soldiers.)

Perhaps the political class is right about foreign policy. Why don't they take their case to the public that will pay the price? They don't have to. The current corruption of our political system allows them to run an unpopular foreign policy with impunity.

The truth is, we no longer have a functioning representative democracy in our land. The people want disengagement: pollster Scott Rasmussen has found that the only two countries most voters agree should be defended by the U.S. are Canada and Great Britain. But these views go unpronounced in the halls of power, because those who exercise that power have become a class unto themselves, impervious to the sentiments and pressures of the benighted many. As Andrew Jackson predicted, "the more secure an office holder, the more his interests would diverge from those of his constituents."[10] By discarding the quintessentially Jacksonian practice of rotation in office, we have inherited a Congress that is free to flout the opinions of the folks back in the district. After all, what are they going to do about it: run against the frank-cranking, staff-fattened incumbent? Lotsa luck.

In 1788, the New Yorker Melancton Smith said that representatives "should be a true picture of the people; possess the knowledge of their circumstances and their wants; sympathize in all their distresses, and be disposed to seek their true interests."[11] Does this describe your congressman? Secure in the fort of Washington, accumulating a pension that dwarfs those of civilian retirees, he may breeze into the district every other Saturday for a faux-folksy "town meeting" at which he will exhibit an almost tearful solicitude for the cares and opinions of constituents whose names he does not know. They will complain about "the government" and he will lend a sympathetic ear, but even the most sincere and decent congressional careerist cannot escape the realization that the system's degeneration has created two classes: Us and Them. The rulers and the ruled.

Madison, who more than any other man can be honored as the father of the Constitution, foresaw the potential of an arrogant protected Congress. But his faith reposed in a watchful people:

> If it be asked what is to restrain the House of Representatives from making legal discriminations in favor of themselves and a particular class of society? I answer, the genius of the whole system, the nature of just and constitutional laws, and above all the vigilant and manly spirit which actuates the people of America, a spirit which nourishes freedom, and in return is nourished by it.[12]

A vigilant people is the palladium of liberty. But we have not been vigilant enough.

CHAPTER THREE

"SAY ANYTHING, DO ANYTHING, SPEND ANYTHING": THE CONGRESS WE'VE GOT

How dire is our situation?

For starters, we do not have anything resembling competitive elections at the congressional level.

In 1996, 296 incumbents who had served more than one term sought reelection. Of these, 289 (98 percent) won. Of the 88 freshmen seeking reelection, 75 won. The 1998 results set records for incumbent security. Of the 401 incumbents seeking reelection, 395 won, for a record high reelection rate of 98.5%. Most faced no serious challenger, so the average margin of victory soared to 40 percentage points.

Even in 1994, the re-election rate for incumbents was 90 percent. Incumbents averaged 64 percent of the vote, meaning that in the most anti-incumbent congressional year in modern memory, the average margin of victory was a landslide.

A challenger has a better chance of striking it rich at the race track than he does of defeating an incumbent congressman. Reelection rates soared to 98 percent in 1986 and 1988, and in elections throughout the 1990s, reelection rates have been above 90 percent. In 1996 the average vote taken by challengers running against incumbents was a pathetic 34 percent in Senate elections and 33 percent in House elections. These are not the signs of a vital democracy. In fact, political analyst Charles Cook wrote in *Roll Call* in 1997, "About 240 House members, making up about 55 percent of the House, couldn't lose reelection if they tried."[1] He was underestimating the case.

Political scientists have remarked often upon the seeming paradox that while Americans give Congress exceedingly low grades, they send their own representatives back to office with fabulously high margins of victory. Explanations for this disparity vary. Certain defenders of the status quo suggest that Americans are simply unsophisticated: children, really, who imbibe demagogic denunciations of the institution of Congress but who nurture a deep and abiding and thoroughly deserved love of their own congressman.

In 1996, pollster Rasmussen found that "most Americans want to replace the entire Congress and start from scratch...only 28% would vote to re-elect the entire Congress. Twice as many (55%) would vote to replace all incumbents."[2] Seven weeks later, these fed-up voters reelected 95 percent of those incumbents. The people, it seems, are mad as hell, and they intend to keep right on taking it.

At least that is the gloss applied by the media. But as we shall see, the real reasons are somewhat more complex.

The only congressional races worthy of the name are usually those for "open" seats, or districts in which no incumbent is running. Open seats are, as a rule, far more competitive than those closed due to incumbency power. In 1996, the average margin in an open-seat race was between 15 and 20 percent — not exactly neck-and-neck, but a 58-42 percent defeat is a lot closer than the typical incumbent-challenger margin, which frequently is so large as to recall the farcical Eastern Bloc ratifications of the Communist era.

The economist Alexander Tabarrok found that between 1960 and 1990, "house seats switched party 5.0% of the time when an incumbent ran and 25.7% of the time in an open election. In the Senate, parties rotated 15.5% of the time when an incumbent ran but 42.7% of the time when the election was open."[3]

To recharge our democracy, therefore, a way must be found to multiply the number of open seats. The best way to accomplish a consistently high number of vacant seats is through term limits.

The death of rotation in office has had disastrous consequences. Today's House may contain people of great ability, but talented newcomers are directed to the back bench, where they must sit for several terms, vote as party leaders instruct, and wait until a string of retirements and deaths opens up positions in the lower leadership. After waiting and toeing the line for ten years, will they still be representative?

Despite the reforms of the 1970s and 1990s, power in the House remains centralized. The system is seniority-based and hierarchical; a freshman had little influence in Newt Gingrich's universe. The proof was in the pudding of the 1996 elections.

Of the nineteen people in "leadership" positions in the House, thirteen were unopposed in their primaries, while the others faced only token opposition. Their average vote in the general election was 66 percent, to 30 percent for the average second-place challenger. The two most powerful, Gingrich and Gephardt, were first elected in 1978 and

1976. Most power in the House rests with those who run the full committees. Of the 20 committee chairs and 20 senior Democrats on those committees, 28 faced no primary opponents and ten faced token opposition; the other two easily defeated challenges. All 40 of these men swept to victory in the general election, with an average vote of 65 percent, to an average for their leading challengers of 31 percent. The 40 averaged 24 years in the House.[4]

They have been in the House a long time, and expect to stay as long as they choose. After a quarter century in the Beltway, and with no real risk of defeat at the ballot box, why should we expect them to be representative? Their arrogance is nicely demonstrated by the redoubtable Henry Hyde, Judiciary Committee chairman and House lifer, who, exasperated by arguments for term limits and against professional politicians, asked, "Is running a modern complex society of 250 million people and a $6 trillion economy all that easy?"[5] No, thankfully, it is not easy to "run" a society and economy. These are, ostensibly, private realms: even the most zealous Communist bureaucrat in the old Soviet Union would gasp at Mr. Hyde's grasp. He really thinks that he and his 534 fellow wise men "run" our lives, our affairs, our pocketbooks. Is there a better advertisement for term limits? (The Nobel Laureate Friedrich Hayek had the answer to Mr. Hyde: "It is an illusion to believe that the people, or their elected representatives, can govern a complex society in detail."[6] Much less "run" things.)

The seniority system guarantees that those members of Congress most removed from the private sector are precisely those who wield the most power within the institution. Is it any wonder that voters complain that the congressional leadership is hopelessly out of touch? One of the more interesting post-career reflections was made by Senator George McGovern, who served three terms representing South Dakota. After retirement, Senator McGovern operated a hotel in Connecticut, which failed. "I wish that someone had told me about the problems of running a business," he mused. "I have to pay taxes, meet a payroll — I wish I had a better sense of what it took to do that when I was in Washington."[7]

The only way Senator McGovern could have gotten that "better sense" of what it's like to make a business succeed would have been by returning to South Dakota as a private citizen after a term or two. McGovern's plaint was anticipated two centuries ago by John Lansing, a delegate to the Constitutional Convention, who advocated term limits before the New York ratifying convention. "By mingling with the people," spoke Lansing, "they may recover that knowledge of their interests, and revive that sympathy with their feelings, which power and an exalted station are too apt to efface from the minds of rulers."[8]

This exalted station is maintained by a variety of means.

The most obvious advantage of incumbency is, fittingly, porcine: the pork that members of Congress, especially those in the majority party, can dish out to hungry special interests back home. Any illusions that the "revolutionaries" swept onto Capitol Hill by the 1994 GOP wave would swear off pork were shattered by 1996. For example, just five weeks before Election Day, 1996, the House shoveled $3.3 million for a courthouse annex in the district of freshman Phillip English (R-PA), an alledged fiscal conservative. English won, narrowly.

Does pork matter? Do these millions upon millions, which in the aggregate become billions upon billions, of dollars of unnecessary spending actually help their congressional procurers? Unfortunately, the answer is yes.

Twenty-five years ago the political scientist David Mayhew wrote, "How much particularized benefits [i.e., pork projects] count for at the polls is extraordinarily difficult to say, but it would be hard to find a Congressman who thinks he can afford to wait around until precise information is available. The lore is that they count."[9]

The lore is right. In the 1970s, Congress Project researchers took a sample of first-term representatives and grouped them according to the amount of federal spending that flowed to their districts. "Those with the least federal spending added 4.6 percent to their original victory margins when they sought reelection," wrote the researchers. "The next group, with more federal spending, received a 6 percent hike in the victory margin. The lucky ones who procured the most local public works added a whopping 8.9 percent to their share of the vote."[10]

Further evidence of the profits of pork comes from a study by Robert M. Stein of Rice University and Kenneth N. Bickers of Indiana University. In examining the 99th and 100th Congresses, Stein and Bickers concluded that "voter awareness of new projects in their district increases the probability of voting for the incumbent House member by 9.7 percent."[11]

Even the most untutored House member understands the implications of these studies. Pork equals votes. If one wishes to make the House a career, then one had best start bringing home the bacon. In a study of the 100th and 101st Congresses, Stein and Bickers found that vulnerable incumbents — specifically those members last elected in an open-seat race by a narrow margin — disproportionately secure pork early in their terms. The reason is simple:

> While only a minority of incumbents typically face quality challengers, high levels of new awards early in the Congressional term reduce the likelihood that incumbents will face quality challengers in the subsequent primary or general election.[12]

A pork-fattened incumbent scares off potential challengers. We are left with a depleted treasury and a national epidemic of electoral romps and no-contests that have turned our political life into a depressing farce. For while representatives and senators dip freely into the pork barrel to enhance their reelection prospects, with each greedy handful they have constructed the mammoth central government against which they so hypocritically rail every election year. Missouri Senator John C. Danforth, a term-limits advocate who voluntarily retired from the chamber, says, "the growth and cost of government has skyrocketed as congressmen say anything, do anything, and spend anything to get themselves elected."[13]

The eminent political scientist Richard F. Fenno, Jr., in his classic study of House members, *Home Style* (1978), profiled the prototypical House careerist, whom he called Congressman E. The perhaps not-so-eminent Congressman E was not native to his district; "I'm not a politician," he pleaded, with some justification. He was a businessman who had done some "speaking in praise of the free enterprise system" and was recruited by other local businessmen to run for office. He won, in a competitive district, and continued to do so: "I always win by less than 55 percent," he told Fenno, and the closeness of his races marked him as not so typical.[14]

Congressman E's first focus was constituency service, which, as Fenno writes, "is totally nonpartisan and nonideological. As an electoral increment, it is an unadulterated plus."[15] Fenno sought to calculate the electoral benefit of such service: "If we equate constituency service with 'the power of incumbency,' our best present estimate is that incumbency, or extra constituent service, adds an *average* of 5 percent to a House member's electoral total."[16] (This was 20 years ago; the figure is undoubtedly higher today.)

The congressman knew this, and acted upon that knowledge. "The biggest part of getting reelected is casework," he told Fenno. "I have the best case workers anywhere, in the district and in Washington."[17]

As for those speeches Congressman E gave in the good old days, the ones extolling the virtues of free enterprise: they were gone with the win. "I've been very successful in getting things for the district," he boasted. "Before I was elected, there were exactly seven miles of interstate highway built in this district. Now, just look at that vista up and down I-40. 'Brought to you by courtesy of your member of Congress, the O'Connor highway.'"

After bragging that the dams and bridges and buildings he had brought to the district had given him whatever electoral security he had, Congressman E had the audacity to add, "My main issue is inflation and holding down the cost of government spending." He found the hypocrisy easy to swallow. "We've been so successful at getting money for this district — the year-by-year graph for FHA [Farmers Home Administration] money goes shooting up — that I'm embarrassed to mention it. My opponent will accuse me of talking out of both sides of my mouth."[18]

His opponent would also lose.

Term limits will not change human nature. They will alter the incentives to which members of Congress, who after all are only human, will respond. If Congressman E could not make the House a home, he would have had far less incentive to spend his workdays draining the treasury of money for election-enhancing projects in his district. Perhaps, in his two or four or six years in office, he might even have found time to act upon the principles he had enunciated before he joined the reelection rat race.

Three political scientists at the University of Rochester, John M. Carey, Richard G. Niemi, and Lynda W. Powell, found that term limits at the state level have significantly reduced pork-barrel spending. They write:

> Term limits decrease the time legislators spend on
> activities for which they are roundly criticized —
> most notably the time they devote to securing pork
> for their districts. Consistent with this result, term-
> limited legislators report placing higher priority than
> do their non-limited counterparts on the needs of the
> state as a whole and on the demands of conscience
> relative to more narrow district interests.[19]

Stein and Bickers emphasize that pork-barrel projects benefit an incumbent only if his or her constituents know who the benefactor was. Certain antediluvian legislators have been in Washington so long that bridges and schools and government buildings back home bear their names: Senator Strom Thurmond's name covers half of South Carolina, and western Pennsylvanians ride on the Bud Shuster By-Way, named for the ethically challenged chairman of the House Committee on Transportation and Infrastructure.

But those pork providers not lucky enough to have a turnpike namesake have plenty of other ways to get the word out, thanks to the hapless taxpayer. The commonest way is by taking advantage of the franking privilege, which allows members to use the mails free of charge for "official business." Alas, the most official business of most congressmen is getting reelected: the frank has become an invaluable weapon in the incumbent arsenal.

In theory, the frank is unobjectionable. As Thomas Jefferson remarked, communication between the people and their representatives should be "free, full, and unawed by any" in order to "give the will of the people the influence that it ought to have."[20] (The frank works only one way, however: the citizen must affix a stamp to his letter.) In any event, the frank bears little if any resemblance to the original Jeffersonian ideal. Less than ten percent of franked mail spending is dedicated to responding to communications from constituents — the only legitimate use of the frank. The other 90 percent is devoted to "campaign propaganda paid for by the taxpayer," as former Senator David Boren (D-OK) complained.[21]

The volume of outgoing mail from the House rises by as much as 75 percent during election years; the purpose of this epistolary blizzard is clear. As Rep. Morris Udall (D-AZ) once said, "As chairman of the Commission on Congressional Mailing Standards, I have often been appalled by the way some Members have perverted the frank. There can be no doubt that by the use of slick, highly targeted mailings many Members have greatly enhanced their chances for reelection."[22]

Stories of frank abuse are legion. There was the congressman from New York who mailed 180,000 letters announcing...a new bench at a bus stop. There was the statewide mailing by Senator Rudy Boschwitz (R-MN) asking Minnesotans to come to the state fair and visit "Rudy's Super Duper Milk House." Congressman Craig James (R-FL) refused the 1990 pay raise of $7,100 and sent 312,000 letters trumpeting the fact

— thus costing the taxpayers $78,000.[23] Responding, in its own fashion, to public outrage over the torrential outpour of franked mail suspiciously close to Election Day, Congress in 1981 banned mass mailings of 500 letters or more within 60 days of an election. This led to a proliferation of mailings of 499 pieces.

The amount of money a member may spend on franked mail is determined by the number of addresses in his district; the average per member is now over $100,000 and climbing, which means that a congressional office can send out approximately one million pieces of mail a year. Not suprisingly, the Republicans have demonstrated no inclination to curb the abuses of the frank that were so pervasive under the Democrats. And why should they? The goal of a congressional candidate, writes David Mayhew, is "to disseminate one's name among constituents in such a fashion as to create a favorable image but in messages having little or no issue content."[24] It is the rare congressman indeed who sends a mass mailing to declare himself on a matter of great controversy; it is far safer to take credit for the new bench on the bus route. As Charles Babcock wrote in the *Washington Post*,

> Both parties teach new members that there are three rules for getting reelected: "Use the frank. Use the frank. Use the frank." It would be funny if it wasn't taxpayers' money and degrading to the whole institution.[25]

During the past decade, members have begun patronizing innovative mailing-list vendors to ensure that those one million missives wind up in the right hands. According to authors Larry Sabato and Glenn Simpson, the House has used taxpayer dollars to help one vendor make its lists accessible in a more user-friendly format. In 1991, Sabato and Simpson report, the House Administration Committee:

> granted Aristotle (a private consulting firm) a $250,000 development loan to transfer its database lists onto CD-ROM format. By the following summer fifty-six legislators had bought Aristotle CD-ROM disks for the total sum of $250,000.[26]

Sophisticated and pricey consultants customize mailing lists for their congressional clients. Constituents are divided into such subgroups as the elderly, Jews, pro-life, military retirees, or a thousand and one other cells. They receive mail that the computer deems "appropriate" for them.

We are a long way from Mr. Jefferson. The frank was designed so that a yeoman on the frontier could write his representative with his insights and the representative could write back. Today, almost all congressional correspondence is written by staff members. Frequently, even the signature is bogus, the high-class forgery of an autopen machine.

The result is an almost wholly illusory contact between members and citizens. One vendor of sophisticated mail management software boasts,

> If you do your homework on the off-years and know your constituency, you won't really have to run a full-blown campaign. With members who use our software, no one can ever say that they are not in touch with their constituents.[27]

But what sort of "touch" is this, when citizens are reduced to mere strips of paper on a computerized mail list? It is factitious, inauthentic, and deeply cynical. And given the technology at hand, and the possibility of lifetime careers in Congress, it is also inevitable.

The explosion of direct mail has widened the gap between the number of voters contacted by mail by incumbents and the number contacted by frank-less challengers. In 1994, for example, 63 percent of voters received mail from incumbents, while only a quarter of voters heard from challengers.[28] Because in 1977 the Congress decided that it would fund with taxpayer money unlimited long-distance telephone service for congressional offices, three times as many voters say that they have talked to a member of an incumbent's staff as have talked to a member of a challenger's staff.[29] (And the challenger has to pay the phone bill out of his own pocket.)

Free mail is only one tool in the belt of the perpetual congressman. Fax machines crank out puffery day and night, as taxpayer-funded press flacks write up their bosses with a reverence right out of *Lives of the Saints*. Television and radio studios are available to members at no cost to themselves. It's a good investment: in 1994, 33 percent of voters said that they'd heard the incumbent on the radio, while only 18 percent had heard the challenger. Sixty-one percent had seen the incumbent on television; 34 percent said that they had seen the challenger.[30]

Members are informed that the congressional recording studios are strictly for purposes of informing people in the home district about legislation and not, absolutely not, absolutely positively not, for campaign purposes. Wink wink, nudge nudge. In fact, the shows beamed back to the taxpayers are full of vapid happy-talk intended to make the incumbent more popular with the voters. *Congressional Quarterly* profiled one Republican freshman, Rep. Kenny Hulshof of Missouri, who eked out a victory in 1996 over a 20-year incumbent Democrat. Congressman Hulshoff had quickly learned the First Commandment of the House: Get Reelected. He says his goal in using the Capitol's broadcast facilities is "to help educate the folks back home on what we do, to make Washington more user-friendly," and to this end he gives out tips on such vital matters as how to get tickets for tours of Washington. It's warm and fuzzy and designed to prolong a budding careerist's career.[31]

World Wide Web sites dedicated to the greatness of Senators and Representatives have proliferated. They contain a vast array of information, including position papers, bills that a member has sponsored or cosponsored, and biographical information. Staffers regularly update the sites. In 1996, CompuServe offered free sites to incumbents and challengers alike, but the Federal Election Commission nixed the idea. In a letter to CompuServe, it stated,

> The Commission still concludes that your proposed gift to Federal candidates of valuable services which enable them to communicate with voters and advocate their candidacies would constitute in-kind contributions to those candidates and would be prohibited.[32]

Thus it is legal for incumbents to use taxpayer dollars to promote themselves on the Web, but it is illegal for a challenger to receive a contribution that would allow him to do the same thing. No wonder establishment reformers point to the FEC as one of their proudest creations.

A congressman without a staff is as lost as an actor without a director and scriptwriter. A large staff of ghostwriters, press flacks, caseworkers, legislative aides, and support people are the cornerstone of the Incumbent Party. Their salaries footed by the taxpayers, congressional staff direct their energies to one purpose above all: make the boss look good.

When Richard F. Fenno was researching his classic *Home Style*, one congressman told him, "What political scientists have to understand is that an incumbent congressman can get reelected by the services he is in a position to do for people." Fenno provides a good working definition of constituent service:

> Many activities can be incorporated under the rubric
> of "district service," or "constituent service," but the
> core activity is providing help to individuals, groups,
> and localities in coping with the federal government.
> Individuals need someone to intercede with the bu-
> reaucracies handling their veterans' benefits, social
> security checks, military status, civil service pension,
> immigration proceedings and the like.[33]

These services are performed by the staff, though the member of Congress gets the credit. And there are plenty of staff to go around. Though senators functioned without personal staffers until 1885, and House members until 1893, today's Congress is dominated by its employees. The personal staffs of representatives have ballooned from a total of 870 in 1930 to 2,441 in 1957 to about 7,500 today; over that same period, Senate personal staffs have expanded from 280 to more than 4,000.[34]

Syndicated columnist Robert D. Novak describes the changes he has seen since he came to Washington in 1957:

> Few members of Congress employed a press secre-
> tary. Nearly all readily responded to phone calls from
> a low-level AP reporter without an aide asking what
> he wanted. With fewer staffers, lawmakers did much
> of their own work. At night on his typewriter, Sen.
> Everett McKinley Dirksen wrote summaries of ev-
> ery bill reported by every Senate committee.[35]

Novak's description seems almost idyllic to us today: a sweet and wistful picture of a world long gone. Staffers today draft bills, negotiate with other staffers, and often instruct their bosses how to vote. Their loyalty is to their boss, not to his constituents; they work tirelessly to promote his good name and prospects for reelection. After all, his defeat translates into their unemployment — which is one reason why staffers are among the most vehement foes of term limits.

To foster the illusion of rootedness, representatives establish district or regional offices. Like the size of personal staffs, the number of district offices has exploded in recent years. In 1964, only four percent of House members listed more than one district office. Today, multiple district offices are the rule. (The average is 2.4 district offices per member.) In 1972, 23 percent of personal House staff worked in district offices; by 1994, 47 percent labored in the district.[36]

What do these district office workers do? The World Wide Web page of a randomly selected congressman, Rep. Joe Knollenberg (R-MI), explains:

> Should you have any questions, concerns, or problems in dealing with any entity of the federal government, please feel free to call my district office. Members of my staff would be happy to assist in locating Social Security or veteran benefit checks, or dealing with the Immigration and Naturalization Service. Additionally, they can also serve as liaisons between you and virtually any other federal agency.

This is wholly unremarkable: banal, even boring. But for a congressman, it's better than a million dollars in the bank.

District-office workers spend almost all their time on casework. Such constituent service is understandable, as the expansion of the federal government over the last 65 years has entangled us all in a nightmarish bureaucratic web. Who hasn't experienced a problem in dealing with the government, whether it's a lost social security check or a delayed visa or a friendly inquiry from the IRS?

But who created the bureaucratic Leviathan? Incumbents have found that constituent service is an excellent way to bolster their reelection prospects. A survey of senior congressional staffers found 56 percent naming constituent service as the most important factor in boosting a legislator's political support. The member's legislative record, by contrast, was chosen by just 11 percent.[37] Another survey, this one done in the mid-1980s, asked congressional administrative assistants whether their bosses thought that constituent service enhanced their election chances. Only two of 102 replied that it did not have a significant electoral effect. The detailed responses of the other 100 are instructive:

- My God, that's why we're here. We're the only office on the Hill with 24-hour turnaround. (One congressman) was defeated because of a six-month turnaround.

- Yes. In our first election we had a majority of only (less than 500) votes. This year we had a 70 percent majority, which is reflective of service to the district.

- You're elected to be a legislator, but casework and projects keep you elected. People in the district expect you to represent them in their dealings with the bureaucracy. Our prime responsibility is to see them and attend to their problems.[38]

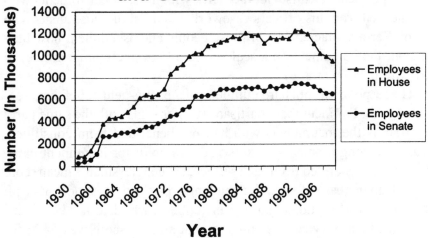

Employees in the House of Representatives and Senate 1930-1997

Congressman Henry Hyde, the aforementioned 12-term veteran who regards the citizens of the United States as mere names in phone books, was blunt in his assessment of the value of constituent service:

Again and again, I will tell you why you have a leg up: good constituent service, accessibility and availability. You ought to have a leg up. You have made

> an investment challengers never make. I will not
> apologize for that.[39]

Hyde is right that constituent service is "an investment challengers never make." Challengers are in no position to dispense favors like manna from heaven. They have neither a taxpayer-financed staff nor free mailing privileges. They cannot buy voters with other people's money. Unless they are exceedingly well-financed, they can only sputter and mumble as the incumbent rails against bureaucracy and unresponsive government. Meanwhile, the incumbent profits from government ineptitude, as lost social security checks and fouled-up visa applications lead a steady stream of supplicants to his door — and a steady stream of grateful voters back out again.

Several recent studies have tried to quantify the advantage of which Congressman Hyde is proud. Many have found it to be substantial — and daunting for potential challengers. (Those who "never make" the investment of winning, in Hyde's gracious formulation.) In 1988, an anonymous House member, curious about the impact of his casework, provided political scientist George Serra with a list of constituents who had benefited from his office's casework and a list of constituents who had not. Serra contacted 419 of those people and asked them how they felt about the incumbent on a scale of zero (extremely unfavorable) to 100 (extremely favorable).

The respondents put hard numbers on the long-held belief that casework matters. For incumbent partisans (respondents with the same party affiliation as the incumbent) who had not benefitted from constituent service, the congressman's mean score was 66.0; for incumbent partisans who had benefitted from such service, the congressman's mean score was 76.8, an increase of 10.8. For challenger partisans (respondents with different party affiliations than the incumbent) who had not benefitted from constituent service, the congressman's mean score was 54.7; for challenger partisans who had benefitted, the mean score was 73.4, an increase of 18.7. Finally, Independents who had not benefitted from constituent service gave the congressman a mean score of 57.2; Independents who had benefitted gave him a mean score of 73.4, an increase of 16.2.[40]

So constituent service does more than just shore up your base; it also greatly improves your approval rating among Independents and those belonging to other parties. Indeed, while the average approval ratings given by incumbent partisans (66.0) and challenger partisans (54.7) were considerably different among those who did *not* benefit from constituent service, that gap was almost erased among constituents who *had* benefited from constituent service (76.8 to 73.4). Moreover, *challenger* partisans who had benefited from casework actually gave the congressman a higher evaluation (73.4) than did incumbent partisans who had not (66.0). Thus, the key to approval lies not in ideology or effective representation but rather in casework. Favors trump principles at election time.

There is even a spillover effect from casework. Using an econometric model, Serra found that "respondents who can recall having friends and/or relatives with satisfactory casework experiences are more favorable in their evaluations of the incumbent than other respondents."[41]

Favorable evaluations translate into votes. An American National Election Study found that, of voters who contacted their representative for constituent service and were "very satisfied" with the result, 64.7 percent voted for the incumbent, 32.3 percent did not vote, and just three percent voted for the challenger.[42]

We are now seeing this taxpayer-funded casework translated into hereditary seats, handed not to blood relatives but to favorite staffers. Former congressional staffers, already in tune with the Beltway and out of touch with the people, are a large source of candidates. Some incumbents even time their retirement announcements close to candidate filing deadlines so that a favored staffer can prepare for an election before anyone else knows the seat will be open. Representative Ron Dellums (D-CA), a 14-term incumbent, took it a step further, making a surprise announcement in late 1997 that he would retire in mid-term, sticking taxpayers with the cost of a special election and giving a twelve-year veteran of his staff a head start on the campaign. With his enthusiastic backing, the former staffer won the low-turnout special election a few months later, and can be expected to hold the seat until she dies or picks an heir.

No wonder casework has come to dominate many congressional offices. Reforming entitlements, rethinking the U.S. government's role in the world, and rejuvenating our lethargic democracy would be hard work; powerful interests might be offended. How much better for the member of Congress — and how much worse for the republic — to ignore the maladies that afflict our body politic and act instead as an ever-grinning ombudsman, tracking down lost pension checks and churning out press releases advertising the fact. How sad that a great body —

the people's house, the repository of the dreams of self-government —
has fallen to such a low estate.

As Harvard political scientist Morris Fiorina writes,

> Improved public policy is a goal that most congress-
> men favor. But reelection is certainly a more impor-
> tant goal. And when given sixteen or eighteen em-
> ployees to allocate as they see fit, congressmen quite
> naturally put the lion's share to work on the most
> important thing, reelection, while perhaps reserving
> a few for secondary matters such as formulating our
> country's laws and programs.[43]

No matter how much we wring our hands or entreat our legislators
to be worthy of their offices, it shall ever be thus — unless we remove
the reelection incentive. Term limits, then, is the keystone of all political
reform.

Even reform as fundamental as the size of government. Fiorina
writes,

> Congress does not just react to big government — it
> creates it. All of Washington prospers. More and
> more bureaucrats promulgate more and more regu-
> lations and dispense more and more money. Fewer
> and fewer congressmen suffer electoral defeat. Ele-
> ments of the electorate benefit from government pro-
> grams, and all of the electorate is eligible for om-
> budsman services. But the general, long-term wel-
> fare of the United States is no more than an inciden-
> tal by-product of the system.[44]

In a pathbreaking series of books and articles, Fiorina argues that
the growth of government, the expansion of constituent service, and the
record-high congressional reelection rates are interrelated. Fiorina writes:

> In the postwar period, we have seen both the decline
> of the marginal district and the expansion of the fed-
> eral role and its attendant bureaucracy. I believe that
> these two trends are more than statistically related.

An institutional change — the growth of the bureaucracy — has encouraged behavioral change *among
congressmen,* which in turn has encouraged behavioral change among some voters.[45]

Fiorina posits that elected officials are like everyone else: they wish
to improve their current circumstances or, if that is not possible, make
sure that those circumstances do not deteriorate. They tend to do what
will help them get reelected; that is, what will improve their standing
with the voters.

Members of Congress can engage in two types of activities, says
Fiorina: the programmatic (introducing legislation, campaigning for its
passage) and the nonprogrammatic (procuring pork, constituent service).
The former can be controversial; unless a member represents a homoge-
neous district, his programmatic activities are likely to lose him the support of some bloc of voters. And given that legislation usually bears
many fingerprints, it may be hard for him to take credit for success.

By contrast, nonprogrammatic actions are noncontroversial and
usually enjoy widespread support. It's easy to claim credit for a new
bridge, especially with a fax machine spitting out press releases. And
who can oppose helping Aunt Lucy get her social security check? These
acts create a reservoir of good will and an appearance of nonpartisan
benevolence.

As a result, a member has two incentives when drafting a bill. First,
the broader and vaguer the legislation, the more difficult it is for voters
to find it objectionable. Second, broad and vague legislation opens up
great opportunities for expanded constituent service and the resultant
favorable image. Fiorina explains:

> The nature of the Washington system is now quite
> clear. Congressmen earn electoral credits by estab-
> lishing various federal programs. The legislation is
> drafted in very general terms, so some agency, ex-
> isting or newly established, must translate a vague
> policy mandate into a functioning program, a pro-
> cess that necessitates the promulgation of numerous
> rules and regulations and, incidentally, the trampling
> of numerous toes. At the next stage, aggrieved and/
> or hopeful constituents petition their congressmen

to intervene in the complex (or at least obscure) decision processes of the bureaucracy. The cycle closes when the congressman lends a sympathetic ear, piously denounces the evils of bureaucracy, intervenes in the latter's decisions, and rides a grateful electorate to ever more impressive electoral showings. Congressmen take credit coming and going. They are the alpha and the omega.[46]

The recipients of all this gratitude and all those votes are simply following the advice of the 16th-century political theorist Niccolo Machiavelli: "A wise prince will seek means by which his subjects will always and in every possible condition of things have need of his government, and then they will always be faithful to him."[47]

The wise princelings of Congress have discovered a way to expand the federal bureaucracy, and thus opportunities for constituent service, while at the same time avoiding any threat of aspersion or blame: they delegate congressional power to the unelected. This makes electoral sense to a careerist politician; alas, it is a constitutional insult.

The Constitution is very clear about where the power to make laws resides. Article 1, Section 1, reads: "All legislative powers herein granted shall be vested in a Congress of the United States, which shall consist of a Senate and House of Representatives." The need for such strict delineation and division of power was explained by James Madison in *The Federalist Papers*:

> The accumulation of all powers, legislative, executive, and judiciary, in the same hands, whether of one, a few, or many, and whether hereditary, self-appointed, or elective, may justly be pronounced the very definition of tyranny.

George Washington, in his Farewell Address, in which he instructed posterity on the precepts of republican government, advised officeholders:

> to confine themselves within their respective Constitutional spheres; avoiding the exercise of the Powers of one department to encroach upon another. The spirit of encroachment tends to consolidate the Pow-

ers of all the departments in one, and thus to create whatever the form of government, a real despotism.[49]

Heedless of the fathers of our country and our constitution, the Congress has ceded much of its lawmaking power to the executive branch and unelected regulators, who create rules and regulations that are often far more complicated and sweeping than what originates in Congress. In congressional testimony, Jerry Taylor of the Cato Institute described the incentives that drive the delegation of the lawmaking power:

> One of the main reasons Congress delegates is to manipulate voter perceptions. Delegation allows legislators to represent themselves to some constituents as supporting an action and to others as opposing it. As former [Environmental Protection Agency] administrator Lee Thomas described delegation under the Clean Air Act, "Everybody is accountable and nobody is accountable under the way [Congress] is setting it up, but [the legislators have got a designated whipping boy.[50]

(Or as the ever-relevant Machiavelli advises, "princes should let the carrying out of unpopular duties devolve on others, and bestow favors themselves.")[51]

The Congress that creates these elephantine bureaucracies and cedes power to them runs for reelection by decrying those very same bureaucracies. Henry Hyde tells partisans of term limits: "Professionals, my friends, will run this Government. Only they will not be elected, they will be the faceless, nameless, try-to-get-them-on-the-phone, unaccountable permanent bureaucracy."[52]

Mr. Hyde is in the curious position of blaming Dr. Jekyll. He defends careerist legislators as veritable safeguards, protecting constituents from the capricious tyranny of those very same bureaucracies that Hyde and his colleagues have created and endowed with delegated powers.

Nevertheless, the lamentations over the tyranny of the bureaucracy are real: the scope of this tyranny has been measured by Clyde Wayne Crews, Jr., of the Competitive Enterprise Institute. In 1997, off-budget regulations cost $688 billion, which is 40 percent of the federal budget.

These regulations cost the typical American family $6,875 in 1997. And despite the hooey about the era of big government being over, the 1996 *Federal Register*, which contains the rules promulgated by federal agencies, was the second-fattest register in the last 10 years.[53]

We must "make Congress directly accountable for every dollar of costs unelected agencies impose on the public,"[54] writes Crews. Until we get a citizen Congress, however, our legislators are likely to keep on passing the buck, and reaping their rewards in votes.

The cynical game of delegation has one purpose — getting reelected — and only the drastic alteration of incentives known as term limits is going to halt this undemocratic perversion.

There is one other culprit in the case of vanishing competitive districts, and this, too, would be arrested — though not eliminated — by term limits. It is the practice of gerrymandering, or drawing congressional districts in such as a way as to protect either incumbents or parties. Ironically, the gerrymander takes its name from one of the Founders, Elbridge Gerry of Massachusetts, an eloquent critic of the Constitutional Convention's failure to codify term limits. ("By this neglect [of rotation] we lose the advantages of that check to the overbearing insolence of office which by rendering him ineligible at certain periods, keeps the mind of man in equilibria, and teaches him the feelings of the governed, and better qualifies him to govern in his turn.")[55]

The party that controls a state legislature redraws the state's congressional districts every ten years. Whereas once, districts tended to have natural boundaries — county lines, rivers, city limits — today, high-priced consultants use computer models to carve out districts that resemble snakes, palm trees, and other exotica. The purpose is to create districts that contain far more registered voters of your party than of the other party. To do this, you must concede a certain number of seats to the other party: thus a typical state legislature may allocate 60 percent of its congressional districts to the dominant party, 30 percent to the out-party, and maybe one in ten seats will be a tossup. In most districts, the majority party will win year after year. And since it is exceedingly rare for an incumbent to face a serious primary challenge, not only will the same party usually win year after year, the same *person* will win year after year. And that's how competitive districts vanish.

The House of Representatives is hardly at the mercy of the state legislatures, though. By doling out billions of dollars to state governments each year, a state's congressional delegation exerts tremendous influence over the state legislature. When, every ten years, it comes time to redraw districts, state legislators are likely to remember which veteran House members bring home the pork — and they will give them the safest possible district. States in pursuit of federal loot have an incentive to protect the most senior members of their delegation: they want the federal spigot to keep flowing. As a result, concludes political scientist Edward R. Tufte, "A major element in the job security of incumbents is their ability to exert significant control over the drawing of district boundaries; indeed, some recent redistricting laws have been described as the Incumbent Survival Acts."[56]

The Center for Voting and Democracy has described the way the gerrymander works:

> Every ten years, legislative districts are redrawn to create safe districts for incumbent politicians and their parties. Not only that, but generally these lines are drawn by the politicians themselves, using sophisticated software to surgically map districts down to the household level — surely a case of the fox guarding the hen house. We like to think that "we the voters" pick our representatives, but it's increasingly true that the politicians choose their voters by gerrymandering safe districts for themselves. In most legislative districts, voters have little choice but to ratify the status quo by voting for the "Untouchable" politician or party from their district, or not voting at all.[57]

Rob Richie of the Center has gone so far as to opine that most congressional elections are decided every ten years, during redistricting. The fix is in. To borrow their pungent phrase, today's politicians choose their voters rather than submit to the democratic indignity of having the voters choose them.

Obviously, term limits will not end partisan politics — they are not intended to. The parties will still press their advantages in state legislatures when it comes time to carve up the map. But some things *will* change. There will be no pork-hauling war horses to protect. A congressional delegation of citizen-legislators will be less obsessed with grabbing for federal money: after all, a major reason for the pork barrel is that it enhances reelection prospects, and term limits would alter these incentives. And at the state level, citizen-legislators will be less beholden to party leaders, and therefore less willing to gerrymander. As we shall see later in this book, one consequence of term limits at the state level has been an increased independence among members; they are more willing to buck party leadership on matters of principle. As we shall see in 2002, when 18 state legislatures do their first redistricting under term limits, citizen-legislators are far less likely than careerists to deface the maps of their own states, to raze the mountains and fill the seas and erase county lines in the service of party. Perhaps someday Elbridge Gerry will be remembered more for his trenchant remarks on representative government than for the travesties of party politics that bear his name.

CHAPTER FOUR

"A PERSON WHOLLY DIFFERENT": THE TERM LIMITS SOLUTION

Let us be clear. However tempting it may be to shout, "Kick the bums out!" the character (or lack thereof) of the current members of Congress is not the cause of our distress. Merely changing captains and officers on the ship of state is not enough when that ship is sinking. The ship itself — the institutional framework of Congress — must be repaired. The incentives to which members of Congress respond must be changed if our reformation is to be anything more than cosmetic.

Mounds of empirical evidence show us just what a difference term limits can make. Even under the current system, with its skewed incentives toward careerism, new members of both parties compile voting records that differ sharply from those of their elders.[1]

For one thing, junior members are less profligate with the public's money. For instance, a 1998 study by the National Taxpayers Union found junior Republicans in the House voted for 6.9 percent less spending than did their senior Republican colleagues; in the Senate, junior Republicans voted for 9.4 percent less spending than did their elders. Another study using National Taxpayers Union scores found that in every year between 1978 and 1990, those members who had served more than 12 years in the House received worse ratings from the frugal NTU than did those who had served less than 12 years. This was true of both Democrats and Republicans.

Scholar James L. Payne argues that members of Congress exist within a "culture of spending."[2] It is a verifiable proposition that the *longer* one spends in Washington, the *more* one spends in Washington. As Payne discovered, almost every witness before congressional committees testifies in favor of spending *more* money on the program in question. Virtually no one exerts pressure for parsimony. As a result, Payne observes, "the longer a congressman serves in Congress and is exposed to pro-spending stimuli, the more in favor of spending he becomes."[3]

Payne's book, *The Culture of Spending*, was published in 1991, at the height (or nadir) of Democratic control. Could it have been that the

Democrats, grown slothful and spendthrift by so many years in power, were responsible for this wasteful culture, and that the Republicans would air out the staleness and start things afresh?

From the evidence, the answer is a loud and dispiriting *No*. The vaunted Republican Revolution of 1994 can only be judged a failure, and the blame for that failure must be placed at the feet of its senior members. Aaron Steelman of the Cato Institute examined 31 key votes from 1995-1997, years of GOP ascendancy. "In nearly every case," Steelman found, "junior Republicans [House members with six years or less experience and Senators who had served for 12 years or less] favored fiscal discipline in far greater numbers than did senior Republicans."[4] The 31 votes were on proposals ranging from the slashing of corporate welfare to the elimination of subsidies for the tobacco and sugar industries to a congressional pay raise. Again and again, junior Republicans voted for fiscal restraint, while senior Republicans, immersed in the culture of spending, voted to empty the exchequer.

Yet we may be sure that if these junior members stick around long enough, they, too, will become part of the semi-permanent governing class. Time dampens firebrands; the self-preservation of a congressional lifer demands that he purge himself of idealism. In the heady wake of the 1994 elections, House Majority Leader Dick Armey (R-TX) said, "If we Republicans can straighten out the House, then I think maybe the nation's desire for term limits can be diminished."[5]

Well, they didn't, and it isn't.

And the reason why the Republicans have not diminished the public's desire for term limits is, to engage in what might seem like circular reasoning, because they themselves are not term-limited. The system will not, because it can not, produce the kinds of citizen-legislators who can get our republic back on track. Absent term limits, we are condemned to an unending series of pork-hoarding, free-spending, responsibility-sloughing solons whose first loyalty is not to their constituents or the nation but to themselves: to their own survival.

The economist and philosopher Friedrich Hayek, author of the classic warning against totalitarianism, *The Road to Serfdom* (1944), cut to the heart of the matter in his book *Law, Legislation, and Liberty* (1973). Hayek anticipated the failure of a careerist-led Republican Revolution to slim our overgrown state:

For the task of laying down the limits of what government may do clearly a type of person is wanted wholly different from those whose main interest is to secure reelection by getting special benefits for their supporters. One would have to entrust this not to men who have made party politics their life's concern and whose thinking is shaped by their preoccupation with their prospects of reelection, but to persons who have gained respect and authority in the ordinary business of life and who are elected because they are trusted to be more experienced, wise and fair, and who are then enabled to devote all their time to the long run problems of improving the legal framework of all actions, including those of government.[6]

A Hayekian cure requires a rotation in office by citizen-legislators; what the Republicans gave us was more of the same old malady.

We should have seen it coming. While Republicans sometimes talked a good game during their years in the wilderness, their elders were paid-in-full members of the Incumbent Party.

One particularly egregious example of the gap between careerists and newcomers (and collusion between the senior members of both parties) was the infamous midnight pay raise of 1989, which passed the House in the black of night by a 252 to 174 vote. The pay raise would have been defeated by a 72 to 49 margin if only members with under six years of service had been polled.

The midnight pay raise — which was one of the sparks that kindled the term limits prairie fire — is a splendid example of the Incumbent Party in action. Democratic and Republican leaders demonstrated that their first loyalties were to the Incumbent Party, with fealty to their own branches thereof being somewhat weaker, and as for the voters — well, a few mouthfuls of pork and help locating Grandma's social security check will keep them quiet.

The leaders agreed to a "non-aggression pact," under which the Democratic and Republican congressional campaign committees pledged not to give money to challengers who raised the midnight pay-raise issue. Newt Gingrich was party to that pact; as Eric Felten recounted, "his [1990] opponent, Democrat David Worley, made it the centerpiece of his campaign. Polls showed Worley nearing a major upset. But then his own party's congressional campaign committee cut off his supply of campaign cash. Despite the setback, Worley lost by only 974 votes."[7] The Incumbent Party had saved one of its own — a man who has since repaid that Incumbent Party many times over. (After the midnight pay-raise vote, Newt Gingrich visited the Democratic caucus — and received a standing ovation.)

The decadence of the Incumbent Party is embodied in Pennsylvania Republican Congressman Bud Shuster, a 25-year veteran of the House whom the passage of time has elevated to the chairmanship of the Transportation and Infrastructure Committee — the pigpen wherein pork is carved and served by the ton. Shuster rose through the ranks thanks to his willingness to be a "partisan hatchet man,"[8] according to the studiously non-partisan *Congressional Quarterly's Politics in America*. He quite astutely realized that the path to power required subordinating one's honor to party leadership and one's political principles to political exigencies. Thus, this self-described fiscal conservative produced, in 1998, what Stephen Moore of the Cato Institute called "the most expensive highway bill in history" and "arguably the most irresponsible spending bill to wind its way through Congress in twenty years."[9]

Columnist Robert Novak notes that Gingrich previewed the strategy in his book *Lessons Learned the Hard Way*, where he wrote of the "meritorious" Shuster highway bill. "We were in real danger of looking like a bunch of fools or hypocrites if we turned around and brought out a massive multibillion-dollar, multiyear bill that destroyed the spending ceilings we had just written into law."[10] Thinking time heals all hypocrisy, they waited a year, piled on billions more, and blasted $33 billion beyond the spending limits in the 1997 budget deal.

What's behind the latest bout of profligacy? Novak reported that on top of the hundreds of projects in the bill, "Friends of the (Transportation) committee and House members of both parties facing tough re-election fights get $20 million to $30 million" to allocate in their districts. The Incumbent Party is looking out for its own, with our money. When Mark Twain said "It could probably be shown by facts and figures that there is no distinctly native American criminal class except Congress," he was referring to the petty bribery that lined the wallets of corrupt lawmakers. Today our problem is the diversion of whole arenas of government to serve the political class. Legalized corruption is the core competency of Congress.

Shuster may even have crossed that fuzzy line where the legalized corruption of Congress becomes brazen enough to embarrass his fellow lifers — no mean feat. The House Ethics Committee is investigating the "enormous public appearance problem arising from the tangled web of legislative, political, financial and personal ties" between the congressman and a female lobbyist who was formerly his chief of staff for 22 years. Again, think of the ways this story would differ in a Congress that practiced rotation in office. Obviously, Shuster would have been long gone from office, but the "tangled web" he and his friend have weaved would not have been possible to craft in a mere six years. The ethic complaints allege, among other things, that Shuster and the lobbyist "used their influence to obtain favorable terms [in transportation contracts]" for contributors to his campaigns.[11] Given that his talents were for partisanship rather than statecraft, it is extraordinarily unlikely that Shuster would have become chairman of the committee. Even if he had wanted to, he wouldn't have been able to "obtain favorable terms" for his cronies. (As we shall see later, legislators under term limits are less partisan and thus less prone to rewarding partisanship in others.) Nor would the chief of staff have been able to build her own base of power, for these webs of corruption take years to spin. Finally, because Congressman Shuster would not have been able to dun the transportation lobby to fill his bulging warchest, he might even have faced a challenger. Under the current system, Shuster is regarded as unbeatable, ethics charges and all. He faced no opponent — not even a token Democrat or third-party challenger — in the 1986, 1988, 1990, 1992, and 1994 elections, and won by a three-to-one margin in 1996. The whole sorry scenario befits a banana republic, not the United States of America.

The imperiousness of congressional lifers is nicely — if chillingly — illustrated by a story from 1991. The protagonist was the autocratic John Dingell (D-MI), chairman of a major House committee first elected to Congress in 1955. (He succeeded his father, who had been elected in 1932.) The chairman "ran his empire with an iron gavel," according to *Congressional Quarterly's Politics in America*. He "was known for bullying witnesses and badgering members...[and for] punishing those who dared cross him and bestowing favors on a select few."[12] He was just the sort of monster who is created in a Congress of lifers — and who cannot exist in a term-limited Congress.

Among the chairman's great fears was term limits. He loathed them with every ounce of his being, seeing them — correctly — as the death warrant of his career. In 1991 agents of the chairman informed a family with extensive business interests that federal regulators would be unleashed unless they severed ties with term limits organizations. Throughout his career, the congressman and his fiefdom brooked no dissent.

The threats are not always conveyed in whispers and glares. This same family was attacked on the floor of the House of Representatives by Congressman James McDermott (D-WA), who repeated charges against the family business that even the supposed victim had already admitted to be baseless. A memo was circulated to House Democrats alerting members to the family's support of term limits and noting that they would have business matters before Congress and regulators. Almost overnight, the threatened family halted financial support to term limits. (Previously, it had been the most generous donor.) And who can fault them? That, sad to say, is how Washington works.

Not that most Americans see life on the Potomac through rose-colored glasses. Just for fun, pollster Scott W. Rasmussen asked a representative sample of 1,000 adults if they thought that Microsoft chairman Bill Gates would be treated more harshly by Congress if it were learned that he had contributed to term-limits organizations. (Which he hasn't, to my knowledge.) By a three to one margin (50 percent to 17 percent), Americans expect that Congress would harass Gates, or any businessman who had the temerity to support rotation in office.[13]

The advantages of term limits are not merely theoretical: they are evinced by those members of Congress who, lacking formal limits, have chosen to limit themselves. In significant ways, they are a breed apart from your run-of-the-mill lifer.

Mark Sanford of South Carolina was first elected in 1994 with a three-term limit. He proposed a highway bill that would end the porkfest, and respect federalism by leaving gasoline tax revenue to the states, letting them fund and manage their own road programs. Fat chance in the careerist Congress. Fellow citizen-legislator Tom Coburn of Oklahoma also opposed the spending frenzy. His promised return home by 2000 left the leadership with no leverage: "I'm not going to be here, and there's not one thing I want from this place," said citizen Coburn.[14] They came to Congress from private sector jobs. "We were political neophytes," says Sanford, who was elected in the Republican landslide of 1994.[15] Sanford had been in the real-estate business; he will return to it three terms later.

The differences between self-limited legislators such as Sanford and the typical lifer were limned by *Congressional Quarterly*. For one thing, they are impatient with business as usual; unlike the lifers, they don't have all the time in the world. The self-limiters were the backbone of the effort to oust careerist Newt Gingrich from the speakership. Taking their stand on principle, they had little to lose; as *CQ* reports, "the traditional cudgels House leaders have at their disposal to enforce party discipline — threatening to boot a member off a key committee, for instance — tend not to be effective with the rebels. Most do not serve on major committees, and those who do will probably depart long before they can climb the seniority ladder."[16]

In other words, self-limiters have the liberty of acting upon their consciences. Party whips do not sting their backs. Term limits embolden members of Congress to do the right thing: they needn't pander to the special interests that sustain the lifers, nor must they bow to the pressures of party leaders. When Speaker Gingrich, abandoning yet another promise, pushed for an increase in the budgets for House committees, it was the handful of citizen-legislators among the GOP who prevented it. As one self-limiting congresswoman said of her vote against Gingrich's committee budget boost, "If you're worried about your career and your next race, and you have to worry about NRCC [National Republican Congressional Committee] funding and whatnot, it's much harder to say no" to an importunate leadership.[17] (Much the same script is played out at the state level. The speaker of the Oklahoma House said of term limits: "Junior members, those with less seniority, will be more aggressive...I mean that in a positive sense...They don't sit around and say nothing for two years. They are active and bring their ideas forward.")[18]

Absent the three-term limit, even those who ride into Washington proclaiming their purity end up in the muck. One of Sanford's colleagues in the Class of '94, Zach Wamp of Tennessee, refused to limit himself to a maximum of six years in the House. By the looks of things, he's gotten mighty comfortable. Wamp has become a champion pork-barreler, using his coveted position on the Appropriations Committee to funnel public money to Tennessee. Says Sanford, "We tell him, by the time you get done [on the Appropriations Committee] there won't be any money left."[19]

Wamp has settled in quite nicely. "This is a world filled with power, money, and sex. All the evil spirits lurk in Washington, D.C.," says Wamp, using the lurid language that appeals to the anti-establishment sentiment back home. But in a moment of candor he admits, "This is not a bad way of life."[20]

Incumbents are happy with their handiwork, but the damage being done to the republic is incalculable. And perhaps unforgivable.

Wamp, and the many others like him in the House and Senate, validates the observation of New Yorker Gilbert Livingston, a term-limits advocate in his state's debate over ratification of the Constitution in 1788:

> In this Eden [Washington] they will reside with their families, distant from the observation of the people. In such a situation, men are apt to forget their dependence, lose their sympathy, and contract selfish habits...The senators will associate only with men of their own class, and thus become strangers to the condition of the common people. They should not only return, and be obliged to live with the people, but return to their former rank of citizenship, both to revive their sense of dependence, and to gain knowledge of the country.[21]

We are entering interesting territory here. After all, as political scientist John M. Carey writes, "theories of legislative behavior are firmly rooted in the assumption that legislators' primary motivation is reelection."[22] Those theories need to be updated to reflect the fact that most incumbents need never worry about reelection. They can focus on building their power, by building the power of their government. Take those away and...? What motivation shall take their place? Might it be something as noble as service to one's neighbors, community, and country?

It is the belief of those in the term-limits movement — and this is not a mere leap of faith, for there is mounting empirical evidence — that citizen-legislators will behave much differently than those currently in power. Lacking the desire — indeed, lacking the opportunity, even if the desire is there — of spending a lifetime in Congress, they will have no incentive to pursue those activities, such as tapping the pork barrel and rigging election rules, that only serve to entrench incumbents. Thus term limits will alter James Payne's "culture of spending." A Congress of careerists will *never* deliver the necessary reforms of the Social Security system, the tax system, or U.S. foreign and defense policy; only a Congress of citizen-legislators can do that. For under the current rules, eager idealists too quickly deteriorate into jaded Zach Wamps.

One enduring myth is that congressmen are ultimately answerable to the folks back home: that in the end, they will vote the way their constituents desire because, as the platitude goes, "we have term limits, and they're called elections." Therefore, members are loath to cross the people who may vote them out of office at the next election.

This neatly describes the way things ought to be. Alas, the elaborate incumbent protection system has consigned this particular notion of accountability to hopeless obsolescence. Despite the occasional high-profile issue (late-term abortions, gun control) on which certain members bow to grass-roots pressure, by and large constituents do *not* greatly influence the votes cast by their (putative) representatives in Congress. Robert Bernstein conducted an extensive study of what he termed "the myth of constituent control." He concluded:

> The myth exaggerates and distorts the influence that constituencies have in determining government policy. It exaggerates the influence that constituencies have over their representatives' policy...Constituencies do not control the policies adopted by their representatives...Constituency influence does not flow primarily from electoral threats against those in office, but rather from the initial selection of representatives.[23]

The initial selection, of course, is a burlesque, corrupted as it is by gerrymandering and a host of disincentives that discourage citizens from seeking office.

I have quoted Machiavelli on various points within this text, because as our 20th century winds down, this 16th century philosopher-cynic speaks directly to our predicament. He did not invent dishonest government, he merely described it, and commended the machinations and feints that sustain it to the princes who would take his advice. Holding power — by any means necessary — has become the cardinal rule of our politics, and if that means trashing the Constitution, bankrupting the federal fisc, and making a mockery of the ideal of free and open elections, then so be it.

The pundits like to blame the people for our plight. Some of us don't even bother to vote, after all — but who, really, can be condemned for ignoring the content-free campaigns and lopsided elections choreographed by the two wings of our single Incumbent Party?

Jefferson defined a republic:

> The true foundation of republican government is the equal right of every citizen, in his person and property, and in their management...The mother principle (is) that governments are republican only in proportion as they embody the will of their people, and execute it.[24]

We are no longer a Jeffersonian republic. Nor are we a well-functioning democracy. The Congress represents not the people but the government itself. And the first step — the essential step — toward retaking that government is term limits.

CHAPTER FIVE

CAMPAIGN FINANCE:
THE UN-REFORM

The political class is desperate to deflect voters' attention from term limits and onto mild, meaningless, or downright malevolent reforms. "Campaign finance reform" heads the list. For instance, the president of the League of Women Voters, which has, alas, become embedded within the Beltway establishment, says, "comprehensive campaign finance reform is a real solution to many of the problems that the backers of term limits are seeking to address."[1]

An effort is being made to change the menu — to substitute campaign-finance reform pabulum for hearty and wholesome term limits. Yet, as Missouri Senator John Ashcroft says, campaign-finance reform is "a meager substitute for term limits."[2] It's not even a substitute, really: it serves not to level the electoral playing field but to tilt it as never before, by making it virtually impossible to defeat any incumbent who is not under indictment on the first Tuesday in November.

The pontificators of the *New York Times* editorial page regularly plump for this menu substitution. They concede that "Popular support for term limits is consistently overwhelming,"[3] but, well, the public is a rude and stupid beast, and Congress's failure to pass the term limits demanded by the people is a "triumph of wisdom."[4] Far better, lectures the *Times*, to "reform the campaign finance laws so that challengers and incumbents can compete on a more equal financial basis."[5] The gray lady has tipped her hand with this admonition, as we shall see. Absent a ban on challenging incumbents, congressional lifers would desire nothing so much as "reform" mandating equal spending in House and Senate races — because years of hard evidence shows that about the only way to defeat an incumbent is to outspend him.

This is not to imply that the *Times's* editorialists have any interest in unseating incumbents. As long ago as 1910, in addressing the matter of direct election of Senators (which the *Times* opposed), the paper declared, "Popular elections are for but one or two terms, while the reelections by Legislatures have seated able Senators for fifteen to thirty years, or for life."[6] Senators who serve for life without ever having to face the voters: this may be called several things, but democratic it is not.

Indeed, the *Times's* contempt for democracy is no recent aberration. After all, it opposed woman suffrage until the bitter end — not on respectable federalism grounds, but because the:

> ordinary female temperament does not inspire trust in the solidity of the feminine political judgement... There are altogether too many sobbers and weepers, romantic poets of politics, in the electorate already. To enlarge it by the admission of a whole sentimental sisterhood would be positively dangerous at present.[7]

After all, thundered the future employer of columnist Maureen Dowd, "emotional instability seems a doubtful qualification in the temperament of a voter."[8]

Be the *Times* as it may, the campaign-finance reform being promoted by the political class has four elements: it would place limits upon spending; provide government funding of campaigns under certain conditions; ban political action committees (PACs); and restrict or outlaw "issue advocacy" advertising by labor unions, right-to-life and pro-choice groups, pro-gun or anti-gun organizations, term-limits supporters, and any other group of citizens who wish to weigh in on a congressional race.

Let us take the last first. The attempt to ban "issue advocacy" advertising — that is, ads that are not paid for by the candidates or parties but by interest groups such as those listed above — is a rank violation of the First Amendment, as the Supreme Court will doubtless rule should this tyrannical legislation ever be signed into law.

Wisconsin Senator Russell Feingold, who is a cosponsor, along with Keating Five Senator John McCain of Arizona, of the best-known "reform" bill, has been the target of anti-abortion "issue advocacy." By silencing his critics — to the applause of the elite media and the political class — Feingold would achieve the dream of thousands of arrogant politicos before him. As conservative columnist George Will writes of these mischievously misnamed "reforms":

> [The] premise is that Americans engage in too much communication of political advocacy, and that the

government — that is, incumbents in elected offices
— should be trusted to decide and enforce the cor-
rect amount. This attempt to put the exercise of the
most elemental civil right under government regulation is the most frontal assault ever mounted on the
most fundamental principle of the nation's Founders.[9]

In 1996, Wisconsin may have provided a chilling preview of where
"issue advocacy" reform is headed at the national level. Incumbents succeeded in getting judges to *ban* ads by the Wisconsin Manufacturers and
Commerce, the Sierra Club, and my organization, Americans for Limited Terms, from the airwaves. Free and open speech, indeed. Journalist
Jonathan Rauch wrote in *The New Republic* that these "episodes appear
to be the first such cases of issue advocacy censorship in the country, but
they were not mere flukes." They're a "logical outgrowth" of the "1970s-
style money-regulating model that still, unfortunately, predominates in
the 'reform' community."[10]

A host of practical objections to the establishment's preferred campaign-finance reform abound, in addition to the philosophical one against
public financing: Should taxpayers be forced to subsidize political parties or candidates they may regard as immoral, sinister, traitorous, or just
plain dumb? Thomas Jefferson said, "to compel a man to furnish contributions of money for the propagation of opinions he disbelieves and
abhors is sinful and tyrannical."[11] It was so 200 years ago, isn't it still
today?

But putting aside philosophical scruples, the effect of the ballyhooed
campaign finance reforms would be to protect incumbents, cripple challengers, and reinforce a status quo that reformers claim to abhor. Spending limits, which at first hearing sound impeccable, are an incumbent's
best friend. Says Harvard Law Professor Einer Elhauge, "Any campaign
finance reform that assures equal spending or equal advertising time in
the election helps preserve the incumbency advantage, not eliminate it."[12]

After all, an incumbent already enjoys widespread name recognition and has an arsenal of taxpayer-financed weapons, from the frank to
the pork barrel. Economist Gordon Tullock, a pioneer of public-choice
analysis, has wondered:

why the Federal Government is never mentioned in
debates about campaign finance as the largest cam-

paign contributor. A congressman gets over $500,000 a year to maintain his office. He gets plane trips to his constituents, a TV studio in the Capitol basement, and other perks. Most important, he can pressure government agencies to do special favors for his constituents. An old woman who finds that her pension comes much faster after she calls her congressman is a pretty secure vote.[13]

Indeed, any fair campaign finance regulation would define most personal staff, franked mail, constituent services, and a portion of the incumbent's salary as campaign spending. It would require members to pay market rates for the use of congressional television and radio studios. One estimate pegs the average taxpayer subsidy of congressional reelection efforts at $1.225 million per two-year cycle — and this doesn't include the members-only benefits of the pork barrel.[14]

According to labor-union consultant and term-limits foe Vic Kamber, "complex legislation and labyrinthine state bureaucracies are often beyond the grasp of neophytes."[15] Curiously, the voters — those dullards in the hinterlands who are too dense to understand the workings of a modern legislature — know the score. A 1997 survey by Rasmussen Research found that 72 percent of Americans say that "members of Congress have unfair advantages over people who run against them."[16] Do not hold your breath waiting for our congressmen to "think, feel, reason and act" like their constituents and strip themselves of the frank and other perks of office.

The Federal Election Commission wants no part in regulating the incumbent protection racket. It has evolved a working definition of campaigning as follows: campaigning is anything done by non-incumbents to influence an election. If only an incumbent can do it, it's not campaigning, and thus not subject to regulation.

Even this laxity does not satisfy congressional leaders. For they seek, too, to silence opposition. If the FEC is deferential when it comes to incumbent spending, it is expansive and broad when outsiders dare to mount challenges to sitting congressmen. In 1996, when the AFL-CIO spent heavily on ads critical of Republican incumbents, Speaker Newt Gingrich demanded FEC action. Republican officials filed at least five FEC complaints against the AFL-CIO. Gingrich made the absurd charge that there is "no other group in America which is allowed to coerce people to give money against their own political vote"— forgetting, apparently, his paymaster, the U.S. government.[17]

Democrats use the FEC with the same vigor when it suits their needs. The Democratic Congressional Campaign Committee and a Republican candidate have filed complaints with the FEC against term-limits groups that ran ads informing voters of incumbents' positions on term limits. They did not dispute the accuracy of the ads. Instead, they disputed the right to deliver them.

Any challenger starts out far behind: forbidding him to spend more than the incumbent is virtually a political death sentence. Some reformers propose congressional race spending limits in the $500,000-600,000 range. This sounds like an ample sum; isn't half a million dollars plenty for a candidate to get his message out? Alas, in most cases, no. In 1996, every single House incumbent who spent under half a million dollars won; by contrast, just three percent of challengers who spent under half a million were victorious. An analysis of races from 1986-1994, adjusting for inflation, yields similar results.

The suggested spending limits in the Senate vary, depending upon state size. The McCain-Feingold bill sets the limits between $950,000 and $5.5 million. In 1994 and 1996, every Senate incumbent who spent less than the limit won; every Senate challenger who spent less than the limit lost. Every one. Surely the truth-in-advertising laws should require the McCains and Feingolds and other Beltway reformers to label their spending-limit bills "Incumbency Protection Acts."

There is an inverse relationship between incumbent spending and electoral success. The more an incumbent spends, the worse he does on election day. That seeming anomaly is easily explained: high campaign spending is usually a sign of weakness rather than strength. If an incumbent cannot win a race simply by exploiting all the perks of office, he is probably too vulnerable to win at all. Nevertheless, he will go down spending, and the special interests who have invested in his career will keep his treasury stocked.

By contrast, most challengers enter their races as relative unknowns, given the enormous population (over 500,000) of each congressional district. They profit greatly from campaign spending. Their marginal benefits from each additional dollar spent are still high by the time they hit a ceiling as low as $600,000. Political scientist Larry Sabato writes:

The question is, who would determine the ceilings?

The Congress, of course — a body composed of 535 incumbents who are fervently convinced of the worthiness of their own reelections. It is in their electoral interests to set the ceilings as low as possible. After all, the incumbents already have high name recognition, purchased with lavish spending during previous campaigns, and with hundreds of thousands of dollars of taxpayers' money (via congressional staffs, the frank, mobile offices, constituency services, and so forth during their years in office). The average challenger, then, begins his or her campaign perhaps millions of dollars behind the incumbent in overall real spending. Major expenditures are necessary to compensate and to compete.[18]

Which brings us to another myth of the ersatz reformers: that campaigns are "extravagantly expensive." It is true that formal spending on congressional campaigns *has* increased sharply; in fact, it's risen at the same rate as federal spending since 1978, leaving it at 0.020 percent (that's right, two one-hundreths of one percent) of federal government spending per two-year election cycle.[19] The total of all formal, voluntary spending on congressional races in the 1995-96 cycle was $626 million. If one includes all spending on the presidential campaigns as well, and

Federal Budget and Congressional Campaign Spending

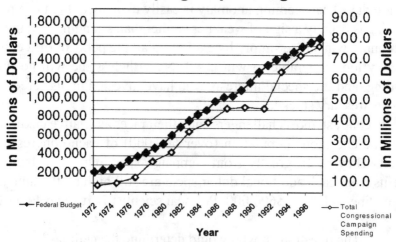

Sources: The Congressional Budget Office and Federal Election Commission

throws in non-regulated spending by the political parties and issue advocacy for good measure, the total was $2.7 billion (which is how much the federal government spends in 15 hours) in the 1995-96 cycle.[20] Curiously, few partisans of campaign-finance reform complain that the federal government is overspending. (One reform proponent admits, "Ultimately, nearly all advocates of reform favor full public financing" — which is wildly unpopular with the public that would be doing the financing.[21])

The 1974 amendments to the Federal Election Campaign Act, passed in the wake of Watergate, clamped a number of spending restrictions upon federal candidates. Most importantly, individual contributions were limited to $1,000 per election, with the primary and general counting as separate elections. (Caps were placed on total spending on House and Senate races, but these were struck down as unconstitutional by the Supreme Court. To get around the Court's ruling, the current proposals

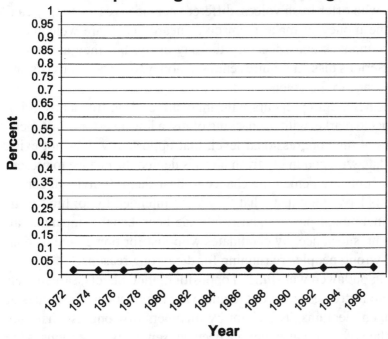

Ratio of Congressional Campaign Spending to Federal Budget

→ Ratio of Congressional Campaign Spending to Federal Budget in Two-Year Increments

Sources: The Congressional Budget Office and Federal Election Commission

make the caps "voluntary," though a series of carrots and sticks make the voluntary aspect rather obscure.)

The $1,000 limit may sound, at first hearing, like a workable way to purge the system of corrupt big money, but in practice it has prevented challengers from raising enough money to mount credible campaigns. An incumbent, after all, begins a race with an operational campaign organization and a database of former contributors. A challenger may need a few wealthy patrons to get his campaign off the ground, but the $1,000 limit ensures that precious few challenges get airborne. (Because candidates may spend unlimited amounts of their own money, the FECA reforms narrow the pool of strong insurgents to the fortunate few: the Steve Forbeses, the Ross Perots.)

Individual contribution limits in congressional campaigns help to keep non-mainstream candidates invisible. A candidate with a visionary but unconventional platform is unlikely to attract the hundreds of $500 to $1,000 donations necessary to mount a credible campaign. Thus, like constituent service, individual donation limits tend to make questions of ideology and principle less important. Candidates who challenge the status quo — who offer fresh voices, different perspectives — simply cannot raise the money to make themselves heard. They are welcome to stand on soapboxes and speechify the day away, but they are utterly harmless. Serious dissent requires enough money to sustain activists and carry a message to the voters.

In business, entrepreneurs with innovative ideas frequently bring their product to market with the backing of just a few investors. In American politics at the congressional level, that opportunity does not exist. The candidate with genuinely fresh ideas is denied the chance to present them; the people are denied the chance to hear them. Individual contribution limits have done just what they were intended to do: limit challenges to incumbent power. The result has been banal campaigns, all image and no substance, by candidates who lust for power and disdain ideas. The wrong people are running for the wrong reasons.

Having outlawed well-funded opposition, incumbents, safe in their invulnerable fortresses, are wont to quote the Founders on the virtues of free and open elections. The claim by members of Congress that they represent the voters because they've been chosen in open elections is the tallest tree of hypocrisy in the Machiavellian forest of modern Washington.

Fifteen-term congressman Bill Clay (D-MO) has said, "If there's one thing we don't need, it's more candidates running for Congress."[22] Thus speaks the arrogance of power, secure in its position, protected by the law. This is what campaign-finance reform delivers. (Clay is echoed by the *Washington Post*'s David Broder, dean of establishment punditry, who says, "Too many people are running for too many offices."[23] The political class and their courtier journalists see the world in much the same way.

The perniciousness of the typical campaign-finance reform proposal was inadvertently revealed by House Democratic Leader Richard Gephardt in a televised 1996 debate. "What we have here," Gephardt blandly declared, "is two important values in direct conflict: freedom of speech and our desire for healthy campaigns in a healthy democracy. You can't have both."[24]

Oh really? The notion that free speech and a vital democracy are incompatible — are mutually exclusive — comes as unwelcome news. Perhaps the solution is to amend the First Amendment, so that it reads:

> Congress shall make no law...abridging the freedom
> of speech...unless such speech might encourage the
> defeat of a Member of Congress.

Gephardt has also advocated shortening the campaign season. He has said that "we should look at a serious limit on the length of campaigns, such as in Great Britain."[25]

The example is apt. For as the *Times* of London recently noted,

> The model of democracy with which Britons are fa-
> miliar emerged in its modern form approximately a
> century ago. It allowed for existing elites and for
> institutions such as the monarchy and Parliament to
> continue in a changed but largely consistent fash-
> ion, despite the evolution to universal suffrage.[26]

No doubt Mr. Gephardt wishes to protect existing elites, himself included. Limits on campaigning would cripple challengers and leave incumbents free to campaign in the guise of "official" business. But then the protection of existing elites is what the establishment's campaign finance reform is all about. Our Founders learned a great deal from Great Britain, which is why they appended a Bill of Rights to our Constitution.

Nothing in world history suggests that the British were right and the Founders were wrong. The pseudo-reformers claim to want to reduce the influence of "big money," but the real target is independent money, which unfortunately is not the big money in American politics today. The biggest money is the $1.7 trillion federal budget, $3.5 trillion per two-year election cycle, controlled by Congress. The next biggest source is the billions of dollars of media coverage, much of it designed to help favored candidates. Interests powerful enough to control large newspapers and television networks, or to have many friends in Congress, have no need to pay their way to get messages to the voters. The backers of further campaign regulation are today's true big money players, the incumbents and their friends in the media, who would win a duopoly if they could shut down the independent dissenters targeted by their proposals.

No restrictions on the rights of citizens to criticize incumbent politicians are acceptable to a free people. Our right to criticize our rulers does not come from any government, and cannot be repealed by any government. As the Founders wrote in the most important document of modern times, the Declaration of Independence: "We hold these truths to be self-evident, that all Men are created equal, that they are endowed by their Creator with certain unalienable Rights, that among these are Life, Liberty, and the Pursuit of Happiness."

Campaign-finance reform, as defined by the elite media and their partners in the seats of power, is a sham that uses high-sounding rhetoric in the service of incumbency protection. It is not an alternative to term limits: it is the negation of fundamental liberties and the subversion of the principle of rotation in office. It is ingenious, we must grant its sponsors that: they have made a skillful play to grab the banner of reform. It is as if the most ravenous wolves caucused and produced a "Sheep Protection Act." You admire their gall, the sheer chutzpah with which they operate, but God save the sheep who fall for the act.

CHAPTER SIX

MEANWHILE, IN THE REAL AMERICA...

The experience of the states, those "laboratories of democracy," confirms the early evidence from Washington. Eighteen state legislatures are now term limited; in 16 cases, it took a voter initiative to impose the limits. Utah's legislature passed term limits to preempt tougher limits threatened by voter initiative; Louisiana's legislature responded to a popular campaign and put a term limits amendment before the voters, where it passed overwhelmingly, as they usually do. In Nebraska, Massachusetts, and Washington state, courts overruled the voter initiatives and struck down limits. As at the federal level, most states — 38 — limit the terms of their executives, the governors.

The initiative, that marvelous tool of direct democracy, is responsible for the revival of rotation in office at the state level. In Colorado, State Senator Terry Considine had introduced term limits bills in the Republican-dominated State Senate, but they went nowhere — "careerists in both parties promptly sunk their knives into it."[1] Term limits would have stayed dead were it not for Colorado's initiative process, and given the lack of any national initiative process, the need for a creative and unorthodox strategy becomes obvious. But more on that in the conclusion.

California political scientist Charles Price, a foe of term limits, asserts that a "substantial turnover in membership could easily weaken legislative leadership. Because legislative leaders will be able to hold office for just a few years, they may not be able to extract campaign contributions from special interests as easily as they have in the past. The diminishing ability of legislative leaders to raise large campaign war chests to give to their party colleagues, will, in turn, weaken their hold over them."[2]

Price rues this development. Party discipline, he believes, is the glue that holds the system together. Those of us who believe that the system is in urgent need of repair beg to differ. We prefer a legislature of men and women sent forth from their communities to act as representatives of those communities, not as catspaws of legislative bigwigs and the lobbyists with the fattest bankrolls. We agree with California Assemblyman Chris Chandler's remark that "If every legislator voted as if this were his last term, this would be a better and more responsive place."[3] Political scientist Linda Fowler, also a term-limits skeptic, argues,

> What you do when you impose term limitations...is to remove the most fundamental incentive for people to engage in political entrepreneurship by saying to potential candidates: "You can take all these risks, but there will be no payoff. You will not be in a position to capitalize on your investment."[4]

We'll set aside the corruption of the word "entrepreneurship": The *American Heritage Dictionary* defines an entrepreneur as "a person who organizes, operates, and assumes the risk for a business venture," which is emphatically *not* what an ambitious politician does.[5] On the larger matter, our political scientist is right: term-limited legislators are not in a position to "capitalize on [their] investment." They cannot build a decades-long career whose final reward is a pension worthy of a sultan. They will be unlikely to parlay their brief tenure into a lucrative lobbying job: after all, pols turned lobbyists are hired for their extensive contacts within the legislature, which is an impossibility given the constant infusion of new faces. (This is what the Founders wanted: James Madison believed that "new members...would always form a large proportion" of the Congress because of frequent elections and the principle of rotation in office, which term limits would restore.)[6]

Fowler is also right to say that term limits removes "the most fundamental incentive" for those who now enter politics: self-aggrandizement. With this incentive — which many of us regard as noxious — removed, our legislatures will attract a different sort of person. Those who dream of spending a lifetime striding the corridors of power, accumulating and peddling influence, imperiously ordering their inferiors hither and yon, will have to find other lines of work.

The careerist Congress has built a palace of perks that rewards long stays in office, from high benefits and pay to lavish pension systems, anchored by the seniority system. The seniority system assures that a certain kind of men will be in control of Congress: men sufficiently obsessed with holding power over others that they will spend a lifetime in pursuit of that power. Such men are not representative of other men, much less of other women. Some 80 years after the amendment creating nationwide women's suffrage, more than half of voters are women. Yet only 13 percent in the House of Representatives are women, and nine percent in the Senate. The 20 full committees, where most of the real power in Congress lies, are all chaired by men, and of the "ranking" Democrats, who would be chairs if party control changed, 19 are men. Three additional women belong to the House's "leadership." In the Senate, 11 of 12 "leaders," all 20 committee chairs, and all 20 ranking members are men. Combined, these 111 people run Congress; five are women. This helps explain why Congress aggressively promotes gender equity intrusions into universities and businesses. They want to turn the light away from the center, and the self-serving rules that assure continued rule by an unrepresentative old men's club.[7]

Twenty-five years ago Pat Schroeder became one of a handful of women elected to Congress, and got this greeting from a veteran incumbent: "Politics is about thousand dollar bills, Chivas Regal, Learjets and beautiful women. What are you doing here?"[8]

Recently Susan Molinari, once the top ranking woman in the House, wrote that she left Congress for network television partly because "Once I hit that woman wall, then how much more could I really have accomplished? I was getting ahead, but I still hadn't been offered a place on any of the really important committees." Her leadership title didn't bring what it could have:

> I was a member of leadership, but I was not, for example, a member of Newt's inner circle, the speaker's advisory group, which is where ninety-nine percent of the decisions that were supposed to be made in leadership meetings are actually formulated.[9]

Molinari correctly notes that this is a bipartisan problem; no woman chaired any committee in Congress from 1976 on under Democratic rule. And with Democratic men holding the "ranking" positions on all but one of the committees, Congress will continue to be run by a men's club no matter which party controls Congress. That they are all men is but a glaring symptom of the central problem with those who run Congress: They are not representative of the American people.

When women run, they do just as well as men. "The problem for women candidates is not sex but incumbency," according to Jody

Newman and the other authors of an exhaustive study of U.S. election results.[10] "Incumbents, most of whom are men, win much more often [about 95 percent of the time] than challengers. For women to have a level playing field, they have to wait for men to retire, resign, or die, and then run for the open seat."[11]

But for whatever reasons, women have been less willing to wait for those open seats, and then wait years more for the possibility of real influence, than men. "In 1994 women made up only 14 percent of the candidates for the U.S. House, and only 16 percent of the all-important open-seat candidates."[18] The old boy's club has rigged the system so that representative Americans don't even run for Congress.

Edward Crane, president of the Cato Institute, calls the current process by which the system produces ambitious careerists "adverse preselection." He writes:

> Those who are successful in the private sector — whether they are entrepreneurs, teachers, computer programmers, or farmers — consider the prospect of running for Congress and realize they'd have to be there 10, 15, or even 20 years to have any real influence under the current regime. They may be perfectly willing to spend some time in Congress as a public service, but not if their time has no impact. They like what they do for a living in the private sector and are disinclined to spend a significant portion of their lives as politicians. Yet those are precisely the kinds of men and women who should be in Congress.[13]

State results validate Crane's diagnosis. The first crop of new state assembly members in California after the passage of the term-limiting Proposition 140 included a pilot, a coroner, a video store owner, a homemaker, an interior designer, a retired teacher, and a retired sheriff's lieutenant — people drawn from the communities they are to serve; talented people from a variety of backgrounds. A few lawyers even made the voters cut. This melange of backgrounds and experience belied the contention of political scientist and term-limits critic Nelson Polsby that a term-limited Congress would be composed of "the rich, the old, and the bought."[14] Rather, it would, like the California Assembly, feature video-store owners and homemakers and pilots — and not Bud Shuster.

The California experience has been extraordinary: some of the post-term limits changes have even surprised the most dedicated advocates. For instance, scholars Kermit Daniel and John R. Lott, Jr. found that "California's legislative term limits have dramatically reduced campaign expenditures,"[15] because the shorter terms sharply reduce the returns a career politician can expect from holding office. At the same time, "more candidates are running for office and races are becoming more competitive."[16]

Professor Mark Petracca has also studied the returns from California. Proposition 140 limited state senators to two four-year terms and assemblymen to three two-year terms. The reform is still green: the first crop of legislators was forced from office in 1996. Nevertheless, the notoriously sclerotic California legislature will never be the same.

Even the harshest critics of term limits concede that the legislature has undergone a facelift that would shame a Beverly Hills plastic surgeon. In 1976, just eight percent of the state's legislators were business owners; in 1995, that figure had tripled, to 23.7 percent. The percentage of legislators with backgrounds in communications and the arts quadrupled. The one occupational group that is found in considerably smaller numbers is attorneys: 36 percent in 1975, down to 22.9 percent in 1995.[17]

The number of women and racial minorities has increased. The number of Hispanics in the California Assembly rose 143 percent between 1990 and 1996. Among Assembly Democrats, the percentage of women has jumped from 17 in 1988 to 40 today.

A legislature that was second only to New York in the permanency of its members has achieved turnover rates that would have pleased John Adams. The percentage of freshmen in the Assembly skyrocketed from a low of 3.75 percent in the apt year of 1984 — yes, that's 3.75, or about one of every 27 seats — to 40 percent in 1996.

Petracca found that from 1990-1996, the transition period during which legislators and voters were adapting themselves to term limits:

- Turnover increased markedly.

- More incumbents lost election bids.

- Those incumbents who won did so by smaller margins.

- The number of uncontested elections dropped significantly.

- More candidates ran for office.[18]

Those who see a Republican tint to term limits can be reassured: in 1996, the first year that limits started removing legislators in Maine and California, the lower houses in both states were recaptured by the Democrats.

From coast to coast, term-limited state legislatures are undergoing similar metamorphoses. A *Wall Street Journal* article in 1997 remarked, "Maine now has its first female House speaker, and half of the legislature's leaders are women, the most ever. Lobbyists find they can no longer rely on old friends."[19] The old boys network has been broken.

Just as nothing concentrates the mind quite like the threat of imminent extinction, nothing focuses the mind of a legislator like the knowledge that the clock is ticking. "Everyone who is here now recognizes that our tenure in the Capitol is limited. The things we do need to matter," says Roy Ashburn, a freshman California assemblyman.[20]

Almost half of the nation's 60 largest cities are also term-limiting elected officials. A study of seven Orange County, California cities that have limited terms since before 1992 found that large majorities of the term-limited officials disagreed when asked if limits "increase the influence of special interest groups in your city" (68.2 percent), "decrease the quality of local government" (77.3 percent), or "lead to a reduction in the quality of individuals running for city council" (86.4 percent).[21]

In California and elsewhere, staffers, lobbyists, and bureaucrats were and are among the most ferocious opponents of term limits. A recent survey by the Council of State Governments found opposition to term limits by 76 percent to 18 percent among state legislators; 82 percent to 6 percent among legislative staffers; and 86 percent to nine percent among professional lobbyists.[22] They are not mistaken in their opposition. Term limits are a stake aimed at the hearts of the careerist legislatures upon which their livelihoods depend. As with a vampire, the stakes are lethal. For as one prominent California lobbyist and foe of limits admits, "lobbyists agree with the advocates for term limits: term limits will disrupt well-settled relationships and make it harder for interest groups to do business."[23]

"Do business": a strange phrase to apply to politics, when you think about it. Might a citizen legislature encourage members of these interest groups to stop lobbying for favors and go home and "do business" of a kind that serves their customers? The executive director of the Ohio affiliate of Common Cause, which has stood with the establishment on this issue, conceded that in her state, "Term limits established a kind of public-interest momentum."[24]

CHAPTER SEVEN

WHERE DO WE GO FROM HERE?: A STRATEGY

The Gingriches and Gephardts — the political lifers who sit atop the seniority system — have shown themselves adept at pursuing phony reforms that diminish electoral competition and perpetuate their own rule. Is it, then, naive to expect them to repeal those measures and open up the political system?

Of course it is. The current system serves them well, even though it serves We the People not at all. They have what most rulers only dream of: immense power with nearly complete protection from competition and accountability. Term limits would divest them of this protection, which is one reason a term-limits amendment is moribund in Congress.

Let's be clear: the term limits movement remains committed to a constitutional amendment limiting members of the House of Representatives to three two-year terms and Senators to two six-year terms. Someday, this amendment may take its proper place, enshrined in the U.S. Constitution, every bit as vital to that document as the Bill of Rights. Someday, but not today, not tomorrow, not even this year or the next.

A Congress of career legislators will never — repeat, *never* — approve an amendment that would usher in a Congress of citizen-legislators. A second method by which the Constitution may be amended — at a convention which can be called by two-thirds of the states — has never been used and likely never will be. The Congress would stall, as the Constitution does not mandate that the convention be convoked within a specified period of time. The rules of the convention would be drawn up by the Congress; the potential for mischief is unlimited. Niggling objections — for instance, that the language differs slightly from one state petition to the next — would permit the pettifogging lawyers who dominate Congress to prattle the issue away. And Congress might also offer incentives (some might call them bribes) to state legislatures to rescind their requests. A constitutional convention, while desirable, is simply not going to be called.

We have learned the hard way that the lifers of both parties speak sweetly and do nothing. Republican leaders, who rode to power behind the Contract with America, torpedoed term limits at every opportunity, while expressing abstract support for this key Contract clause. (The term-limits bill most of them backed in 1995 proposed 12 year limits for both houses of Congress, and actually would have overridden stricter state laws.)

Before the term limits wave washed over American politics, Gingrich referred to himself as a "professional politician."[1] His candor, at least, was appreciated. For Gingrich and the professional pols are part of the problem, not part of the solution. Gingrich's old House ally, ex-Rep. Mickey Edwards (R-OK), says of his former colleague, "He is a major advocate of term limits, but he doesn't believe in them, as far as I know."[2]

Gingrich is not alone in holding this bizarre posture. Those of us in the term-limits movement have met countless politicians who assure us of their undying support for term limits — at least for limiting the terms of everyone else, at some indefinite point in the far future. They tell their constituents that they are as committed to term limits as they are to mom's apple pie, then they vote for watered-down parodies of term limits, fully intending to hold their seats unto eternity.

An analyst in the conservative journal *National Review* noted that the term-limits crusaders of the early 1990s have since split into two camps. Or perhaps it would be more accurate to say that one group has defected from the movement: those who, according to the author, "have seen term limits as a tool to help Republicans gain an edge in Congress." These are the opportunists who latch onto any popular movement, hoping to suck some benefit from it; now that Republicans control the House, and probably will for some years to come, the opportunists have lighted upon other causes. This has left the movement in the hands of those who "have tended to think that term limits themselves will have a direct and positive effect on officeholders."[3] Term limits will, indeed, already are benefiting Ohio and California and Maine and the other 15 states that have rediscovered the revitalizing and revitalized principle of rotation in office.

As the British rock group The Who sang in the 1960s, we won't get fooled again. Career legislators can fill our ears with honeyed words and candied promises, but we know better now. We have learned that only a Congress of citizens can be trusted to create a term-limited citizen legis-lature. Does this sound like a hopeless redundancy? How do we leapfrog the careerists to elect the citizens?

There is a way: it is a time-honored feature of American life. We must transform term limits from an airy abstraction to which any ambitious schemer can give lip-service into a *personal pledge*. When a candidate asks for our vote, we must ask the candidate in return whether he or she plans to be a citizen legislator or a career politician. We must vote for the former. If none of the candidates is willing to renounce careerism, we must recruit candidates who will.

The term-limit pledge is simple. For House candidates it reads:

> I, [name], declare and pledge to the citizens of
> [state]: I will not serve in the United States House
> of Representatives for more than 3 two-year terms.

The Senate version has a two-term limit.

We will ask every candidate for House and Senate to sign the pledge. Our greatest opportunities reside in the 80 or so races that are competitive each election cycle. Given that polling indicates voters are far likelier to cast a ballot for a self-limiting candidate, we expect a healthy number of pledgees. In this way we shall build a citizen legislature from the ground up: district by district, citizen by citizen.

Will the self-limit pledge work? Will it give us a citizen Congress? A survey by Fabrizio-McLaughlin and Associates asked, "Would you be more likely to vote for a candidate who pledges to serve no more than three terms in the House, or a candidate who refuses to self limit?" The responses were:

More likely to vote for self-limiter:	72 percent
More likely to vote for a non-limiter:	10 percent
No difference, or don't know:	18 percent[4]

Candidates read polls. Admittedly, few incumbents will take the pledge. But many challengers will, and given that most seats become open every decade or two — whether through redistricting, the incumbent retiring to accept a high-priced lobbying job in Washington, or a resignation triggered by a felony conviction — we will start filling the Congress with citizen-legislators. Once a district is represented by a term-limited member, it will be tough for a careerist to win that seat.

Voters elected 45 self-limited candidates to the House in 1998. That should rise to about 85 in the 2000 election. The redistricting election of

2002 will produce a bumper crop of open seats *and* citizens bound for Congress. The 2002 election should result in over 130 term limited members. Their presence will alter the institution; their numbers will change the calculus of conventional politics.

Voters will not have a real choice for Congress until a national effort is made to run a slate of citizen candidates more interested in fundamental, structural reform than in the narrow "issues" that dominate public discourse. (Remember flag-burning, a key "issue" of the 1988 campaign?) We need citizen candidates who will come from their districts, rooted in the wisdom and folkways of their people, and return after one to three terms in the United States Congress, giving way to another citizen, and then another, and then another.

"It is a delusion to think that good public servants are a dime a dozen in each congressional district," sneers political scientist Nelson Polsby, who evidently has a low opinion of his neighbors.[5] If only one man in each district of 500,000-plus is sterling enough to serve in Congress, we are indeed in mighty bad shape. But would Dr. Polsby care to argue that, say, Bud Shuster is the finest man in all of Pennsylvania's Ninth Congressional District? Are there no doctors, housewives, business people, artists, farmers, industrial workers, or civic leaders in the entire Altoona area who could do as good a job representing their neighbors as does the ethically challenged Mr. Shuster? I doubt it.

Abraham Lincoln, who served all of one term representing his Illinois district in the House of Representatives, once said, "If our American society and United States Government are overthrown, it will come from the voracious desire for office."[6]

The hunger today is even more ravenous than in Lincoln's time. Our central government has expanded exponentially: opportunities for wielding power, bending others to your will, and enriching yourself and your pet interests are wider than ever before. This appetite for power can never be slaked, but it can be controlled. While we cannot, at present, limit that time by amendment, the self-limiting pledge is the one strategy that promises a representative Congress.

We realize that not everyone who enters Congress does so as a knave. Certainly some come to stay, intending to make the House a permanent home, but others are corrupted by an institutional culture that prizes re-election above all. The self-limit pledge gives voters the chance to head the careerists off at the pass — to respond to the strangulated cry of those congressmen on the verge of becoming lifers: "Stop me before I run again." Okay, we will. And we will once more populate Congress with representatives, not rulers.

Only a term-limited Congress will be willing to confront head on the major issues of the day. A careerist Congress will dilly and dally, temporize and avoid, seeking only its own perpetuation.

So we the people of the term-limits movement will no longer beseech Congress. We will not lobby it, nor will we plead for votes from members who pledge support for some abstract "term limits" but refuse to limit the one term over which they have complete control: their own. Instead, we will work to see that the political class is thrown out, and replaced by citizens who do not need to be lobbied to do what is popular and right.

We have tried the conventional strategy of pursuing a constitutional amendment through the U.S. Congress and found it wanting. Rather we found Congress not wanting any such amendment. From our labors came an insight, however: Politicians who claim to support term limits for others, but won't live by them, are insincere. Term limits are virtuous, and virtue begins at home. Promises to vote for an unpassable amendment are irrelevant.

Restoring representative government in these United States will require a fundamental change in the composition of Congress. Career rulers must give way to citizen legislators. There is no other way. Relying on careerists to revitalize our lagging democracy is an exercise in futility, and futility breeds the corrosive cynicism and distrust that are eating away at the American polity. We must make the noble term "representative" mean something again.

The battle between the permanent political class and the people is about to be fully joined. Term limits will ensure a Congress of citizens, and will begin the renewal of our republic, the rejuvenation of American political life, and the restoration of the Founders' dream. All that is required is for good men and women, good Americans, to act.

RECOMMENDED READING

Gerald Benjamin and Michael J. Malbin, editors, *Limiting Legislative Terms* (Washington: Congressional Quarterly, 1992).

James T. Bennett, and Thomas J. DiLorenzo, *Official Lies: How Washington Misleads Us* (Alexandria, VA: Groom Books, 1992).

James K. Coyne, and John H. Fund, *Cleaning House* (Washington: Regnery Gateway, 1992).

Edward H. Crane, "Reclaiming the Political Process" and Roger Pilon, "Freedom, Responsibility, and the Constitution: On Recovering Our Founding Principles" in David Boaz and Edward H. Crane, editors, *Market Liberalism: A Paradigm for the 21st Century* (Washington: Cato Institute, 1993).

Kermit Daniel, and John R. Lott Jr., "Term Limits and Electoral Competitiveness: Evidence from California's State Legislative Races," *Public Choice* 90 [1997]: 165-184.

Sarah N. Gevers, "Dispelling the Myths: Why Campaign Finance Reform Fails Where Term Limits Succeed," U.S. Term Limits Foundation, *Outlook Series*, Volume VI, Number 1, September 1997.

Bernard Grofman, editor, *Legislative Term Limits: Public Choice Perspectives* (Boston: Kluwer, 1996).

Alexander Hamilton, James Madison, and John Jay, *The Federalist Papers* (New York: New American Library, 1961/1788).

Marta Hummel, "The Empire Strikes Back: A History of Political and Judicial Attacks on Term Limits," U.S. Term

Limits Foundation, *Outlook Series*, Volume VI, Number 2, January 1998.

John L. Jackley, *Hill Rat: Blowing the Lid Off Congress* (Washington: Regnery Gateway, 1992).

James Madison, *Notes of Debates in the Federal Convention of 1787 as Reported by James Madison* (Athens, OH: Ohio University Press, 1984/1840).

Eric O'Keefe and Aaron Steelman, "The End of Representation: How Congress Stifles Electoral Competition," *Cato Institute Policy Analysis*, No. 279, August 20, 1997.

Thomas Paine, *The Life and Major Writings of Thomas Paine*, edited by Philip S. Foner (Secaucus, NJ: Citadel Press, 1974).

Mark. P. Petracca, "California's Experience with Term Limits," U.S. Term Limits Foundation, *Outlook Series*, Volume VII, Number 3, April 1998.

Scott Rasmussen, *The Political Depression* (forthcoming; check *www.portraitofamerica.com* for latest information.)

Mark Sanford, *The Trust Committed to Me* (Washington: U.S. Term Limits Foundation, forthcoming).

Herbert J. Storing, *What the Anti-Federalists Were For* (Chicago: University of Chicago Press, 1981).

George Will, *Restoration: Congress, Term Limits and the Recovery of Deliberative Democracy* (New York: Free Press, 1992).

ENDNOTES

INTRODUCTION

[1] "Term Limits: A Victory for Good Sense," *New York Times,* March 31, 1995, editorial page.

[2] Mark P. Petracca, "Restoring 'The University in Rotation': An Essay in Defense of Term Limitation," in *The Politics and Law of Term Limits*, edited by Edward H. Crane and Roger Pilon (Washington: Cato Institute, 1994), p. 59.

[3] Thomas Paine, "Common Sense," *The Life and Major Writings of Thomas Paine*, edited by Philip S. Foner (Secaucus, NJ: Citadel Press, 1974/1776), pp. 30-31.

[4] Alan Murray, Foreword to Larry J. Sabato and Glenn R. Simpson, *Dirty Little Secrets: The Persistence of Corruption in American Politics* (New York: Times Books, 1996), p. ix.

[5] "Deconstructing Distrust: How Americans View Government," The Pew Research Center for the People and the Press, 1988, from the Internet site www.people-press.org, pp. 1-9.

[6] John Mercurio, "For One More Race, the Doctor is In," *Roll Call*, March 19, 1998, p. 14.

[7] George Melloan, "Democracies Also Should Beware of Rights Erosion," *Wall Street Journal*, November 18, 1997, p. A23.

CHAPTER ONE

[1] George Will, *Restoration: Congress, Term Limits and the Recovery of Deliberative Democracy* (New York: Free Press, 1992), p. 110.

[2] Mark P. Petracca, "Rotation in Office: The History of an Idea," in Gerald Benjamin and Michael J. Malbin, *Limiting Legislative Terms*

(Washington: Congressional Quarterly, 1992), p. 27.

[3] Ibid., p. 28.

[4] Ibid., p. 21.

[5] Ibid., p. 22.

[6] *Seedtime of the Republic* (New York: Harcourt, Brace and Company, 1953), p. 141, as quoted by Ronald Hamowy in his introduction to *Cato's Letters* (Indianapolis: Liberty Fund, 1995) p. xxxvii.

[7] Ibid., p. 418.

[8] Ibid., p. 422-23.

[9] James K. Coyne and John H. Fund, *Cleaning House* (Washington: Regnery Gateway, 1992), pp. 110-111.

[10] Adams, "Thoughts on Government," in *American Political Writing During the Founding Era 1760-1805*, Volume 1 (Indianapolis: Liberty Press, 1983), p. 403.

[11] Petracca, "Rotation in Office: The History of an Idea," p. 26.

[12] Max Farrand, ed., *The Records of the Federal Constitution, Volume III* (New Haven: Yale University Press, 1966) p. 621.

[13] Petracca, "Rotation in Office: The History of an Idea," p. 32.

[14] Letter from Jefferson to Madison, December 20, 1787, reprinted in Andrew Carroll, ed., *Letters of a Nation*, (New York: Kodansha International, 1997), p. 77.

[15] Coyne and Fund, p. 112.

[16] Robert Struble, Jr. and Z.W. Jahre, "Rotation in Office: Rapid but Restricted to the House," *PS: Political Science & Politics*, Volume

XXIV, Number 1 [March 1991]: 34.

[17] James Bryce, *The American Commonwealth*, (New York: Macmillan, 1910), p. 9.

[18] Petracca, "Rotation in Office: The History of an Idea," p. 40.

[19] U.S. Term Limits, Washington, D.C.

[20] Letter from Eisenhower to a friend reprinted in Gabor S. Boritt, "Ike Liked Term Limits," *The New York Times*, November 8, 1994, editorial page.

CHAPTER TWO

[1] Richard F. Fenno, Jr., "The United States Senate: A Bicameral Perspective," *AEI Studies* 362, American Enterprise Institute, 1982.

[2] Paul Johnson, *A History of the American People* (New York: Harper Collins, 1997), p. 108.

[3] Richard F. Fenno, Jr., *Home Style: House Members in Their Districts* (Boston: Little, Brown, 1978) p. xi.

[4] Ibid.

[5] *The American Heritage College Dictionary,* Third Edition (Boston: Houghton Mifflin, 1993), p. 1375.

[6] John Adams, Op. cit., p. 403

[7] Coyne and Fund, p. 7.

[8] Steven Kull, I.M. Destler, and Clay Ramsay, "The Foreign Policy Gap: How Policymakers Misread the Public," The Center for International and Security Studies at the University of Maryland, October 1997.

[9] "George Washington's Farewell Address," in *Two Centuries of U.S. Foreign Policy: The Documentary Record*, edited by Stephen J. Valone (Westport, CT: Praeger), pp. 6-7.

[10] Petracca, "Rotation in Office: The History of an Idea," p. 37.

[11] Herbert J. Storing, *What the Anti-Federalists Were For: The Political Thought of the Opponents of the Constitution* (Chicago: University of Chicago Press, 1981), p. 17.

[12] James Madison, "Federalist No. 57," in *The Federalist Papers* (New York: New American Library, 1961/1788) p. 353.

CHAPTER THREE

[1] Charles Cook, "Payraise Fallout More Likely to Come from GOP Ranks than Voters," *Roll Call*, September 29, 1997, p. 6.

[2] "55% Want to Replace Entire Congress," Rassmussen Research press release, September 4, 1997. Rasmussen's Web Page contains many other survey results from his organization, including that only 25 percent of voters think their representative is the best person for the position in the district; most do not trust their own representative to do the right thing most of the time, and only one in three believes that our government reflects the will of the people. What looks like popular support in landslide elections is something closer to the opposite. Entrenched incumbents who have deterred or hobbled all serious challengers coast to unpopular reelection. (www.portraitofamerica.com)

[3] Alexander Tabarrok, "Term Limits and Political Conflict," in *Legislative Term Limits: Public Choice Perspectives,* edited by Bernard Grofman (Boston: Kluwer, 1996), p. 237.

[4] Calculated from information in Michael Barone and Grant Ujifusa, The Almanac of American Politics 1998 (Washington: National Journal, 1997).

[5] Rep. Henry Hyde, *Congressional Record*, March 29, 1995, p. H3906.

[6] F.A. Hayek, *Law, Legislation and Liberty*, Volume 3 (Chicago: University of Chicago Press, 1979), p. 144.

[7] Will, p. 200.

[8] Michael J. Malbin, "Federalists v. Antifederalists: the Term-Limitation Debate at the Founding," in *Limiting Legislative Terms*, p. 58.

[9] David Mayhew, *Congress: The Electoral Connection* (New Haven, CT: Yale University Press, 1974), p. 57.

[10] Mark Green, *Who Runs Congress?*, 3rd edition (New York: Viking, 1979), p. 57.

[11] Robert M. Stein and Kenneth N. Bickers, "Congressional Elections and the Pork Barrel," *Journal of Politics* 56, no. 2 [May 1994]: 392-93.

[12] Kenneth N. Bickers and Robert M. Stein, "The Electoral Dynamics of the Federal Pork Barrel" *American Journal of Political Science* 40, no. 4 [November 1996]: 1300.

[13] *Limiting Presidential and Congressional Terms*, p. 20.

[14] Fenno, *Home Style*, p. 103-104.

[15] Ibid., p. 104.

[16] Ibid., p. 108-09.

[17] Ibid., p. 108.

[18] Ibid., p. 106.

[19] John M. Carey, Richard G. Niemi, and Lynda W. Powell, "The Effects of Term Limits on State Legislatures," presented at the annual

meeting of the American Political Science Association, San Fransisco, August 1996, p. 35.

[20] James T. Bennett and Thomas J. DiLorenzo, *Official Lies: How Washington Misleads Us* (Alexandria, VA: Groom Books, 1992), p. 38.

[21] Ibid., p. 41.

[22] Ibid.

[23] Ibid., p. 49.

[24] Ibid., p. 53.

[25] Ibid.

[26] Sabato and Simpson, p. 233.

[27] Irwin B. Artieff, "Franking Law Revisions Approved by Congress: Senate Mass Mailings OK'd," *Congressional Quarterly* 39 (October 18, 1981), p. 234.

[28] Gary C. Jacobson, *The Politics of Congressional Elections,* 4th edition (New York: Longman, 1997), p. 100.

[29] Ibid.

[30] Ibid.

[31] Jeffrey L. Katz, "Studios Beam Members from Hill to Hometown," *Congressional Quarterly*, November 29, 1997.

[32] Steven Hayward and Allison R. Hayward, "Gagging on Political Reform," *Reason,* October 1996, p. 26.

[33] Fenno, *Home Style,* p. 101.

[34] Norman J. Ornstein, Thomas E. Mann, and Michael J. Malbin, *Vital*

Statistics on Congress, 1995-1996 (Washington: Congressional Quarterly Press, 1995), table 5-2.

[35] Robert D. Novak, "What a Change 40 Years Makes," *Washington Post,* May 12, 1997, p. A19.

[36] Ornstein, Mann, and Malbin, tables 5-3 and 5-4.

[37] Eric Felten, *The Ruling Class: Inside the Imperial Congress* (Washington: Regnery, 1993), p. 192.

[38] Bruce Cain, John Ferejohn, and Morris Fiorina, *The Personal Vote: Constituency Service and Electoral Independence* (Cambridge, MA: Harvard University Press, 1987) pp. 78-79.

[39] Rep. Hyde, *Congressional Record,* March 29, 1995, p. H3906.

[40] George Serra, "What's In It for Me? The Impact of Congressional Casework on Incumbent Evaluation," *American Politics Quarterly* 22, no. 4 [October 1994]: 403-408.

[41] Ibid., p. 412.

[42] Douglas Rivers and Morris P. Fiorina, "Constituency Service, Reputation, and the Incumbency Advantage," in *Home Style and Washington Work: Studies of Congressional Politics,* edited by Morris P. Fiorina and David W. Rhode (Ann Arbor: University of Michigan Press, 1989), pp. 25-26.

[43] Bennett and DiLorenzo, p. 56.

[44] Morris P. Fiorina, *Congress: Keystone of the Washington Establishment* (New Haven, CT: Yale University Press, 1977), p. 49.

[45] Morris P. Fiorina, "The Case of the Vanishing Marginals: The Bureaucracy Did It," *American Political Science Review* 71, no. 1 [March, 1977]: 177. Fiorina's arguments cogently outline how professional legislators maintain power at the public's expense. Like many of his colleagues, however, he disdains term limits. In *Divided*

Government he predicted that members of term limited legislatures would "have less time to accrue technical expertise," legislatures would shift into Republican hands and be populated by more lawyers and extremists of "both ends of the political spectrum." None of his predictions have come true. In California, where term limits have taken effect, and Michigan, where term limits are rotating out all state legislators elected in 1992 and earlier, term limits have opened the door to technical experts who have worked in the private sector, not changed the party in power (Democrats lost power, but regained it, in California, and Republicans in Michigan have maintained their slight majority) and given women and minorities a much stronger foothold in the legislatures than in the past. He also refers to citizen legislators as "amateur legislators," revealing an implicit bias against those outside of professional politics. See Morris Fiorina, *Divided Government* (Needham Heights, MA: Simon & Schuster, 1996), pp. 53-58. For the effects of term limits in California see Mark Petracca, "California's Experience With Legislative Term Limits," U.S. Term Limits Foundation, *Outlook Series,* Volume VII, Number III, April, 1998. And for Michigan, see George Weeks, "Term Limits Recycle Capitol Insiders," *The Detroit News,* May 19, 1998 at www.detroitnews.com and Steve Harmon, "Term Limits May Open More Doors for Women," *Lansing State Journal,* December 27, 1997.

[46] Fiorina, *Congress,* p. 48.

[47] Niccolo Machiavelli, *The Prince and the Discourses* (New York: Modern Library, 1950), p. 39.

[48] Madison, "Federalist No. 47," *The Federalist Papers,* p. 301.

[49] George Washington, "Washington's Farewell Address," in *George Washington: A Collection,* edited by W.B. Allen (Indianapolis: Liberty Classics, 1988), p. 521.

[50] Jerry Taylor, Testimony before the Subcommittee on Commercial and Administrative Law of the House Committee on the Judiciary, September 12, 1996.

[51] Machiavelli, p. 70.

[52] Rep. Hyde, *Congressional Record*, March 29, 1995, p. H3906.

[53] Clyde Wayne Crews, "Ten Thousand Commandments: A Policymaker's Snapshot of the Federal Regulatory State," Competitive Enterprise Institute, January 1998, Executive Summary.

[54] Ibid.

[55] Petracca, "Rotation in Office: The History of an Idea," p. 33.

[56] Edward R. Tufte, "The Relationship Between Seats and Votes in Two-Party Systems," *American Political Science Review* 67, no. 2 [June 1973]: 551.

[57] Steven Hill and Rob Richie, "Reading the Vital Signs of Democracy," on the Web at: http://www.igc.org/cvd/.

CHAPTER FOUR

[1] Unpublished analysis done by John Berthoud, president of the National Taxpayers Union Foundation, on March 5, 1998.

[2] James Payne, *The Culture of Spending: Why Congress Lives Beyond Our Means* (San Francisco: ICS Press, 1991).

[3] Ibid, p. 79.

[4] Aaron Steelman, "Term Limits and the Republican Congress: The Case Strengthens," Cato Institute Briefing Paper, forthcoming, p. 1.

[5] Katharine Q. Seelye, "Term-Limits Gamble," *New York Times*, March 31, 1995, p. A26.

[6] Hayek, *Law, Legislation and Liberty*, Volume 3, p. 30.

[7] Felten, p. 8.

[8] Philip D. Duncan and Christine C. Lawrence, *Congressional Quarterly's Politics in America 1996* (Washington: Congressional Quarterly, 1995) p. 1135.

[9] Stephen Moore, "Knee-capped," *National Review,* March 9, 1998, p. 26.

[10] *Washington Post,* April 2, 1998.

[11] "House Starts Ethics Investigation into Lawmaker's Tie to Lobbyist," *New York Times,* November 14, 1997.

[12] *Congressional Quarterly's Politics in America 1996,* p. 689.

[13] "Americans Think Congress Would Punish Those Who Give to Opposing Campaigns," Rassmussen Research press release, March 12, 1998.

[14] Guy Gugliotta, "GOP Rebels: Older, Bolder, More Influential," *Washington Post,* April 3, 1998, p. A1.

[15] Carroll J. Doherty and Jeffery L. Katz, "Firebrand GOP Class of '94 Warms to Life on the Inside," *CQ News,* January 28, 1998.

[16] Ibid.

[17] Robert Schlesinger, "Term Limits Groups Urge Self-Limits in Tactical Switch," *The Hill,* February 25, 1998, P. 1.

[18] Gary W. Copeland, "Term Limitations and Political Careers in Oklahoma: In, Out, Up, or Down," in *Limiting Legislative Terms,* p. 151.

[19] Doherty and Katz.

[20] Ibid.

[21] Malbin, "Federalists v. Antifederalists: The Term-Limitation Debate and the Founding," p. 57.

[22] John M. Carey, *Term Limits and Legislative Representation* (Cambridge University press, 1996), p. 3.

[23] Robert A. Bernstein, *Elections, Representation, and Congressional Voting Behavior: The Myth of Constituency Control* (Englewood Cliffs, NJ: Prentice-Hall, 1998) p. xiv.

[24] Letter to Samuel Kercheval, July 1816, quotes in David N. Mayer, *The Constitutional Thought of Thomas Jefferson* (Charlottesville: University of Virginia, 1994), p. 13.

CHAPTER FIVE

[1] Becky Cain, "Term Limits: Not the Answer to What Ails Politics," *The Politics and law of Term Limits*, p. 48.

[2] Sarah N. Gevers, "Dispelling the Myths: Why Campaign Finance Reform Fails Where Term Limits Succeed," U.S. Term Limits Foundation, *Outlook Series*, Volume VI, Number 1, September 1997, executive summary.

[3] "Self-Limiting Terms in Congress," *New York Times*, May 16, 1994, p. A10.

[4] "Term Limits: A Victory for Good Sense," *New York Times*, March 31, 1995, editorial page.

[5] "Right Call on Term Limits," *New York Times*, May 24, 1995, p. A20.

[6] "Not a Little Discussion Needed," *New York Times*, November 21, 1910, editorial page.

[7] "No Time for Experiments," *New York Times*, October 26, 1915, editorial page.

[8] "Equality," *New York Times*, October 14, 1915, editorial page.

[9] George Will, "Government Gag," *Washington Post*, February 13, 1997, editorial page.

[10] Jonathan Rauch, "Speech Impediment: Wisconsin's Cheesy Reform," in *The New Republic*, September 1, 1997, pp. 10-11.

[11] Thomas Jefferson, "Statute of Virginia for Religious Freedom," in *The Political Writings of Thomas Jefferson*, edited by Edward Dumbaud (Indianapolis: Bob-Merrill, 1981), p. 34.

[12] Gevers, p. 6.

[13] Gordon Tullock, "The Real Issues," Letter to the Editor, *National Review*, May 19, 1997, p. 6.

[14] O'Keefe, Eric, "The End of Representation: Congress Escapes the Constitution." Unpublished paper. U.S. Term Limits, 1997: p. 27.

[15] Vic Kamber, *Giving Up on Democracy: Why Term Limits are Bad for America* (Washington: Regnery, 1995), pp. 44-45.

[16] "72% Say Members of Congress Have Unfair Advantages over Challengers," Rasmussen Research press release, July 27, 1997.

[17] Transcript from a videotape of Newt Gingrich speaking at a public gathering in Rockford, Illinois, April 11, 1996.

[18] Larry J. Sabato, *Paying for Elections: The Campaign Finance Thicket* (New York: Priority, 1989), p. 22.

[19] Filip Palda, *How Much is Your Vote Worth?*(San Francisco: ICS Press 1994), p. 97.

[20] Ruth Marcus and Charles R. Babcock, "The System Cracks Under the Weight of Cash: Candidates, Parties and Outside Interests Dropped a Record $2.7 Billion," *Washington Post*, February 9, 1997, p. A1.

[21] David Dyssegaard Kallick, "If Campaign Finance Reform is the Beginning, What is the End?" *Social Policy*, Vol. 26, No. 1 [Fall 1995]: 3.

[22] Amy Keller, "Why Fund Study on Why Good Candidates Don't Run?" *Roll Call*, June 30, 1997, p. 8.

[23] Kamber, p. 35.

[24] Gevers, p. 11.

[25] Rep. Richard Gephardt, Testimony on Campaign Finance Reform, November 2, 1995, from the Internet site: wais.access.gpo.gov, pp. 24-40.

[26] "Virtual Democracy: politicians cannot ignore the public desire to participate," *Times* of London, January 9, 1997, editorial page.

CHAPTER SIX

[1] John David Rausch, Jr. and Gary Copeland, "Term Limits in Oklahoma, California, and Colorado in 1990," in *Legislative Term Limits: Public Choice Perspectives*, p. 204.

[2] Charles M. Price, " The Guillotine Comes to California: Term-Limit Politics in the Golden State," in *Limiting Legislative Terms*, p. 130.

[3] Ibid., p. 135.

[4] Linda L. Fowler, "A Comment on Competition and Careers," in *Limiting Legislative Terms*, p. 182.

[5] *The American Heritage College Dictionary*, p. 459.

[6] John G. Kester, "State Term-Limits Laws and the Constitution," in *The Politics and Laws of Term Limits*, p. 109.

[7] Michael Barone and Grant Ujifusa, *The Almanac of American Politics 1998* (Washington: National Journal, 1997) pp. 1570-71.

[8] Pat Schroeder, *24 Years of House Work...and the Place is Still a Mess: My Life in Politics*, (Kansas City: Andrews McMeel, 1998), p. 260.

[9] Susan Molinari, *Representative Mom: Balancing Budgets, Bill and Baby in the U.S. Congress*, (New York: Doubleday, 1998), p. 260.

[10] Richard A. Seltzer, Jody Newman, and Melissa Vorhees Leighton, *Sex as a Political Variable: Women as Candidates and Voters in U.S. Elections* (Boulder, Colorado: Lynne Reinner Publishers, 1997), p. 7.

[11] Ibid.

[12] Ibid.

[13] David Boaz and Edward H. Crane, editors, *Market Liberalism: A Paradigm for the 21st Century* (Washington: Cato Institute, 1993), p. 56.

[14] Kamber, p. 102.

[15] Kermit Daniel and John R. Lott, Jr., "Term Limits and Electoral Competitiveness: Evidence from California's State Legislative Races," *Public Choice* 90 [1997]: 165.

[16] Ibid., p. 192.

[17] Mark P. Petracca, "California's Experience with Legislative Term Limits," U.S. Term Limits Foundation, *Outlook Series*, volume VIII, number 3, April 1998, table 13.

[18] Ibid., p. 19.

[19] Marta E. Hummel, "The Empires Strikes Back: A History of Political and Judicial Attacks of Term Limits," U.S. Term Limits

Foundation, *Outlook Series*, volume VII, number 2, January 1998, p. 42.

[20] Gevers, p. 17.

[21] Mark P. Petracca and Kareen Moore O'Brien, "The Experience with Municipal Term Limits in Orange County, California," in *Legislative Term Limits: Public Choice Perspectives*, p. 299.

[22] Keon S. Chi and Drew Leatherby, "State Legislative Term Limits," in *Solutions*, Volume No. 6, Issues 1, pp. 31-33. The bright news in the study is that in the California and Maine legislatures, where term limits have already rolled out many of the old boys, half of incumbents now support term limits. Still far short of the public's support, but progress.

[23] Elisabeth A. Capell, "The Impact of Term Limits of the California Legislature: An Interest Group Perspective," in *Legislative Term Limits: Public Choice Perspectives*, p. 73.

[24] Gevers, p. 16.

CHAPTER SEVEN

[1] Connie Bruck, " The Politics of Perception," *The New Yorker*, October 9, 1995, p. 50.

[2] Ibid., p. 74.

[3] John J. Miller, " Terminally Inept?" *National Review*, March 9, 1998, p. 48.

[4] Polling data from U.S. Term Limits, Inc.

[5] Will, p. 56.

[6] Paul Jacob, "From the Voters With Care," in *The Politics and Law of Term Limits*, p. 35.

ACKNOWLEDGEMENTS

Howard Rich, president of U.S. Term Limits, proposed two years ago that I write this book to outline why our national government is impervious to positive and popular reforms. It didn't take long to find numerous facts to illustrate the argument; most of the work was not finding evidence, but compressing it into this short volume.

Discussions with dozens of people have helped shape the ideas in the book. David Boaz, Ed Crane, Paul Jacob, Kurt O'Keefe, David Padden, Tom Palmer, Luanne Radel, and Scott Rasmussen provided comments on various drafts of the book. Paul Farago, Stephen Kresge, Ken McConnell, and Bill Wilson provided insights about the severity of the breach between the politicians and the people. Aaron Steelman found strong arguments for "The End of Representation: How Congress Stifles Electoral Competition," a paper we co-wrote for the Cato Institute. I've incorporated some of those arguments here. Bill Kauffman used his keen eye and sharp pen to reduce the length and increase the clarity of the work. Laura Walton Crouch designed the layout, greatly improving the appearance of what I sent her.

The U.S. Term Limits Foundation, Inc., provided considerable research assistance. Sarah Gevers helped with early research that added muscle and avoided errors, and Marta Hummel was indispensable in offering ideas on quotes, charts and tables, editing, and more. David M. Brown made numerous helpful suggestions.

My cousin Kelly O'Keefe and his colleagues Brian Thomson and Karen Smith very generously donated the cover design and artwork.

I'm especially indebted to my wife, Leslie Graves, for improvements to the manuscript, and to her and our children Sara, Kelly, and Colin, for sharing hours of conversation about Congress and government. My parents Don and Mary have more than a parental role in the book and my related political activities. Countless dinner table discussions with their seven children were held with this premise: America is our country, and we share responsibility for who runs our government, and how it is run.

APPENDIX

THE TERM LIMITS CAUCUS

Those citizens elected to serve no more than three terms will form a dynamic bipartisan caucus in Congress. On matters like pay, perks, and pensions, they will find it easy to side with the citizens against the careerists. And on bigger issues from foreign policy to corporate welfare, they will often split with the lifers of both parties running Congress. The voters will finally have some representation in Congress.

This caucus could soon be acting like an informal citizens party, squaring off against the two branches of the Incumbent Party. This historic confrontation can highlight for the whole country that the veterans running Congress hold the interests of government ahead of the public interest.

Even fifty or sixty term limited members will put tremendous pressure on the seniority system. Can it stay intact when so many members have no prospect of chairing a committee during their entire stay? The number of term limited members is likely to exceed the difference between the majority and minority party. Those term limited will have an interest in using that situation to maximize their influence during their limited stay. And the rulers of Congress will have an incentive to bargain for at least some support. A gradual crumbling of the seniority system is easy to foresee. If congressional leaders prefer a more confrontational approach, they risk drawing more attention to the bipartisan Term Limits Caucus, and creating a faster move among voters toward term limited candidates. Either way lies declining power for the political class and more representation for ordinary Americans.

MAKING YOUR VOTE MATTER

Most modern congressional campaigns are designed to manipulate voters. The candidates are not offering their frank opinions for voter acceptance or rejection; they are not asking questions to learn what voters think. Instead, they hire professional consultants who survey voters and find out what people want to hear; they shape their messages to manipulate voter opinions of them. And they study opposing candidates and design messages, whether true or not, to cast their opponents in the worst possible light. That's the ugly anatomy of a modern campaign for a competitive seat.

The consultants are experts in campaigning who will not follow the winning candidate to office. The winner's performance in office has no connection with his statements during the campaign. And as we have seen, once in office, it is very difficult for voters to get rid of a congressman.

It is no coincidence that the candidate messages sound pretty good, if bland; they are a mirror of the popular opinions of surveyed voters in the district. They don't reflect leadership or principle; they reflect opinion surveys and the timid and generic advice of professionals who know lots about elections and little about real people in the district.

This is a predictable consequence of a system where incumbents are entrenched for life. Why would an ambitious candidate take risky or unpopular positions during a campaign? If he has a controversial position, he'll hide it from voters until entrenched in office. Once in, he can vote how he wants with impunity. So the consensus of the hacks who oversee congressional campaigns is: Say what works to get elected; once you're in, you can do whatever you like.

Voters are shown content-free party labels and campaigns designed to obfuscate the records and opinions of candidates. Yet these elections are our last hold on popular control of government. We must find a way to make our votes matter.

That's the purpose of the Term Limits Declaration distributed to all federal candidates by U.S. Term Limits. It is a nonpartisan, independent pledge to serve no more than three terms in the U.S. House of Representatives, or two terms in the U.S. Senate. That's it. No promise to vote this way or that way on any bill or amendment, not even a term limits amendment. No way to duck and dodge and explain away breaking this pledge because others in Congress would not go along. This is a personal pledge about something under the sole and exclusive control of the candidate.

All candidates claim to be citizens, close to the people and sure to stay that way. That's what their consultants tell them to say. But who means it, and who is trying to sneak in as a pretend citizen, only to show his stripes as a career politician later? This Term Limits Declaration separates the aspiring careerist from the genuine citizen. It separates those planning to rule from those planning to represent, and it does it up front, before they are entrenched in office.

If even ten percent of us adopt this filter before considering voting for any candidate, before checking party labels or claimed issue positions, we can weed out the careerists every time there's an open seat, and occasionally when there is a competitive election involving an incumbent not yet permanently entrenched. Avoid the self-serving deceptions of the consultants, and make your vote count. Look for signers of the independent U.S. Term Limits Declaration. Anyone else is a careerist politician on the make.

PARTY LABELS AND RUNNING FOR OFFICE

"The issues...are nonpartisan issues. I'm trying to be as nonpartisan as possible," said Doug Ose, while winning the Republican party line in California's open third congressional district.[1] "There isn't a dime's worth of difference" on social issues between him and pro-life Republican nominee Gex Williams, while on economic issues, the Republican is "to our left," says the Democratic nominee in Kentucky's open fourth district.[2]

These candidates were being unusually honest about something most incumbents have known for years. The party labels don't mean anything. They are also pioneers in another respect: They both won election after signing the U.S. Term Limits Declaration to serve no more than three terms in the House. They ran as citizens, and intend to stay that way. Their real party is the party of the people, the informal party of citizens, that will stand independent of both branches of the Incumbent Party.

---

[1] Green, *Sacramento Bee*, June 4, 1998, quoted in *National Journal's Hotline*, June 4, 1998.

[2] Dana Milbank, Party Crashers, *The New Republic*, June 15, 1998, p. 25.

A century of encroachment by federal and state governments has corrupted America's political parties beyond recognition. Last century rapid rotation in the House meant that the views of candidates would reflect those of the local political party. The parties regularly nominated new people to run for open seats. Small staffs and short stays in Washington left incumbents neither the time nor inclination to lose touch with the people. The power of the political parties was centered in their control of nominations. If the party did not like an incumbent's performance, it could refuse re-nomination, causing involuntary retirement.

Those nominations were made by well-informed party activists in private conventions. Before the importation of the Australian ballot at the end of the 19th century, election "tickets" were printed and circulated by the parties to help their candidates. The states only counted votes.

Then came "progressive" reforms to take the nomination process out of "smoke-filled rooms." Why did the politicians pass these reforms? They didn't like discipline from party officials, and figured they'd have more power and independence facing the voters in primary elections. They were right; incumbents are almost always renominated. Without the discipline of informed party activists who held the power of nomination over their heads, incumbents grew increasingly independent of party activists and the rest of their neighbors.

The parties gradually descended to their current position as conduits for money under the firm control of incumbents. Parties used to be a way for the people to control candidates and incumbents; now they are a way for incumbents to control campaign money and the nominations of other candidates. If you think that the parties stand for something, consider the issue of abortion. Each party's platform takes an unequivocal position, the Republicans pro-life, the Democrats pro-choice. If nominee positions are indistinguishable on foreign policy, crime, and the environment, at least they are different on abortion, right? No. In competitive districts, the party label is no help to voters, even on abortion.

There was a Republican National Committee resolution in 1997 to prevent national party funding from going to candidates who refused to support the popular ban on "partial birth abortions." Various pro-life Republicans argued that such a ban would risk Republican control of

Congress, and that funding should be available to all with the Republican label. They prevailed. Meanwhile, the Democrats were out recruiting pro-life congressional candidates to run in conservative districts. They are more concerned with having a majority to vote for their leaders in Congress than with driving any issue or agenda. Both parties are serving the interests of veteran incumbents by seeing that the parties provide no discipline over candidates, and no guidance to voters.

This approach was made explicit by Democratic Congressional Campaign Committee (DCCC) political director Paul Frick, who told *The New Republic* "The only real litmus test we have is, 'who are you going to vote for for speaker?'"[3]

The party label means nothing precise and often precisely nothing about the beliefs and future behavior of candidates. We cannot blame candidates for recognizing the reality that parties can't control nominations or candidate platforms. In fact, those who claim there is some fundamental difference between the parties are the ones performing a disservice; they encourage voters to stick with one label, which in most districts gives them no real choice in November.

Congress cemented the two leading political parties in place with the election law "reforms" of the 1970s, which created taxpayer funding for their national conventions and presidential campaigns. These two facts together virtually preclude any successful third party in America: 1) the big two are government sanctioned and funded; and 2) they can do nothing to keep anyone from running for nomination under their labels.

Why should a candidate choose another label when the big two come with a stamp of government approval and a built-in base of voters?

There are ways that the parties could be re-privatized and reinvigorated. But what we can do here and now to restore representative government? Serious candidates should run under the party label of convenience in their district. In an inner city, run as a Democrat. In the Rocky Mountain states, most districts will elect only someone with a Republican la-

---

[3] Dana Milbank, Party Crashers, *The New Republic*, June 15, 1998, p. 21-22.

bel. For years in the South, you had to wear the "Democrat" label to be elected.

This is how the party labels work today: A Republican or Democrat is whatever the voters in a district's primary election say. There is no other standard, no set of beliefs, no single belief to define belonging to either party. There are enough obstacles in the fight to restore representative government; on party labels, reformers should go with the flow. They should choose a party like they choose their campaign clothing: Wear whatever label suits the district.

FOR MORE INFORMATION

For information on term limits on Congress, state legislatures, or local officials, contact:

> U.S. Term Limits Foundation
> 1125 15th Street NW
> Suite 501
> Washington, DC 20005
> 800.733.6440
> 202.463.3200
> http://www.ustermlimits.org
> email: admin@ustermlimits.org

To contact the author:

> Citizen Government Foundation
> 504 E. Madison Street
> Spring Green, WI 53588
> 608.588.7748
> http://www.limitedterms.org
> e-mail: eoke@mhtc.net

More copies of *Who Rules America: The People vs. The Political Class* can be ordered from either of the above organizations.

INDEX

F

Fabrizio-McLaughlin and Associates, 71
fascism, 4
fax machines, campaign use of, 29
Federal Election Campaign Act (FECA), 59
Federal Election Commission (FEC), 30, 56-58
federal government, public confidence in, 3
The Federalist Papers (Madison), 15, 38
Federal Register, 40
Feingold, Russell, 54-55, 57
Felten, Eric, 45-46
Fenno, Richard F., Jr., 15, 25, 31
Fiorina, Morris, 36
First Amendment, 61
Forbes, Steve, 60
Foreign Affairs, 4
foreign aid, public attitude toward, 17-18
franking privilege, 27-29, 56
Franklin, Benjamin, 9
freedom of speech, 61-62

G

Gates, Bill, 48
gender equity issues, 64-66
Gephardt, Richard, 1, 9, 22, 61, 71
Gerry, Elbridge, 40
gerrymandering, 40-41
Gingrich, Newt, 1, 9, 22, 46, 49, 56, 65, 71
Gordon, Thomas, 8
Great Britain, campaigning in, 61

H

Hamilton, Alexander, 9
Hayek, Friedrich, 23, 44-45
A History of the American People (Johnson), 15
Home Style (Fenno), 25, 31
House of Representatives
    Bank overdraft scandal, 12
    Ethics Committee, 47
    leadership positions in, 22-23
    number of women in, 64-66
    political party switches in, 22
    Post Office scandal, 12
    proper place of, 15-16
    term-limit pledge for, 73
    turnover rates, history of, 10-13
Hulshof, Kenny, 30
Hyde, Henry, 1, 23, 33-34, 39

I

incumbents
    advantages for, 24
    and campaign finance reform, 58-62
    and constituency service, 33-36, 55-56
    district offices of, 30-32
    misuse of franking privileges by, 27-29, 56
    personal staffs of, 30-33, 55-56
        as potential candidates, 35
    re-election of, 21-22
        and constituency service *versus* legislative record, 34
international political state, 4
isolationism, 17-18
issue advocacy advertising, ban on, 55

J

Jackson, Andrew, 12-13, 18-19
Jefferson, Thomas, 11, 27, 52, 55
Johnson, Paul, 15
junior members, attitudes of, *versus* senior members, 43-45, 49

K

Kamber, Vic, 56
Knollenberg, Joe, 32

L

Lansing, John, 23-24
Law, Legislation, and Liberty (Hayek), 44-45
lawmaking powers, 36-38
    delegation of, 38-39
lawyers, as representatives, 66-67
leadership, congressional, 22-23, 43-45, 49, 64-66
League of Women Voters, 53
Lee, Richard Henry, 9, 11
legislative activities, 36-38
    delegation of, 38-39
legislative behavior, theories of, 50-51
legislative record, *versus* constituency service, and re-election prospects, 33
Lincoln, Abraham, 16, 74
Livingston, Gilbert, 50
lobbyists, 24-25, 49
    opposition to term limits, 68
Lott, John R., Jr., 67
Lott, Trent, 1
Louisiana, term limits in, 53

M

Machiavelli, Niccolo, 38, 51
Madison, James, 11, 19, 38, 64
mail, and franking privilege, 27-29, 56